Thank God For New Churches

Thank GOD For New Churches!

Church Planting — Source of New Life

James H. Lehman

Brethren Press: Elgin, Illinois

THANK GOD FOR NEW CHURCHES

Library of Congress Cataloging in Publication Data

Lehman, James H.
    Thank God for new churches.

    1. Church growth—Church of the Brethren—Case studies.
2. Church of the Brethren—History—20th century.   I. Title.
BX815.L43   1984   286′.5   84-6429
ISBN 0-87178-840-3

Brethren Press
1451 Dundee Ave.
Elgin, Ill.
60120

CONTENTS

FOREWORD

During a recent visit with the Genesis Fellowship in Putney, Vermont, someone was heard to say: "The high point of our life as a new church was the ministry of Jim Lehman when he was here to prepare for his book. He visited us one by one, asking probing questions that had not been asked before and listening with a sharp ear and a sympathetic, caring heart."

This book is a unique ministry that will benefit not only the new congregations featured within its pages but also older congregations that have forgotten the joy of newness, the struggle of growth and formation, and the thrill of enabling new life in the lives of individual persons, families, and neighborhoods.

Here is a collection of stories about people whose lives have changed as they have become part of a contemporary chapter of church history. The groups that are introduced have all come into being since the late seventies, most in the first half of the eighties. They are in diverse geographies from California to Puerto Rico, from the Androscoggin River in Maine to the Caloosahatchee in Gulf Coast Florida. These churches are in new towns and old cities. They are coming out of the rich soil of the many cultures that participate in today's human mosaic in the United States.

Brother Lehman wrote this book because something happened to him as he sensed the excitement of the new Brethren who have appeared at Annual Conference whose witness has begun to touch the more traditional Brethren. He asked to tell these stories because he feels they need to be heard by the whole church. Jim Lehman wonders if a major new movement may be entering the denomination's history, one that will change the Church in important ways. He seeks to discern what people hope to receive from the Christian community, how the good news of Christ's love is heard and received, and the relevance of the New Testament message for our threatening, complex times.

This is an unusual and valuable book for the Brethren and a useful tool for church leaders of other heritages who are seeking ways of communicating the gospel and strengthening the church in this world.

Student pastor Tim Jones was speaking for a growing company of new church leaders when he preached on "Grasshoppers in the Land of Giants" at the fire hall in Lampeter, Pennsylvania. That feeling and that faith are shared by Sadie Kreider, the Busbys, the Riveras, the Kims, and many others whose vision and sense of calling inspire the rest of us.

MERLE CROUSE

St. Cloud, Florida

ACKNOWLEDGMENTS

In the fall of 1982, I traveled across Indiana, Ohio, Pennsylvania, Maryland, and Virginia, looking for people to help underwrite this book. To the twenty-one donors who said yes to my request, I am especially grateful. Your support came at a time when I felt discouraged and alone, wondering if I would ever find backing for my idea. Without your help, this project would never have gotten off the ground.

To Merle Crouse, who after that initial fund-raising phase picked up the project and provided the rest of the money (two-thirds of the total) from an already overtaxed new church development budget and who submitted to many hours of interviews—I say thank you. Without your cooperation, time, and backing, this book could never have been completed.

To Don Shank, who at two crucial moments gave me encouragement and who understood why I undertook this quest—thank you for your vision.

To my wife and children, who stayed at home while I traveled all over the country and who put up with financial hardship when the time needed to finish the book exceeded the budget—thank you for your patience and love.

To Bob Bowman, editor, and Marilyn Nelson, editorial assistant—thank you for your careful work.

To the 260 people I interviewed—thank you for patiently answering my questions, for talking about your struggles as well as your successes, for, in some cases, speaking my language because I could not speak yours, for being willing to trust me and my tape recorder. If the Spirit of God is in this book, it is here because of you.

Finally, to the members of one particular new church (you will know who you are)—I say a special thank you. You helped me to a deeper experience of the presence of Christ and to a new appreciation of the Church of the Brethren.

JIM LEHMAN

CHAPTER ONE
STARTING SPONTANEOUSLY

The new church development movement in the Church of the Brethren began quietly and was hidden in scattered churches and districts as the ministry of Jesus was hidden in obscure Palestinian villages. For several years we did not even know we had a movement. Even today, early in 1984, when the General Secretary of the denomination is saying that new church development is the "new faith frontier for the Church of the Brethren," and there are denominational goals, budget, and staff, the movement has a spontaneous, fruitful, and undisciplined character. This is its chief virtue and validation.

"You plant seed," says Don Shank, describing his experience starting a new church, "and you wait and wait and you think, 'God, will it ever grow? Are we ever going to see the sprouts? Come on, Lord, hurry up! I can't wait much longer!'" The new church he describes is in Cape Coral, Florida. The movement began there.

In 1974 an Ohio Brethren family wrote to I. W. Moomaw in Florida asking him why there was no Church of the Brethren in Naples, Florida, where they had recently moved. Moomaw brought the letter to the district board in June of that year. The district executive was Merle Crouse, who had taken the job two years earlier with the conviction that the Florida/Puerto Rico district had to begin growing or it would eventually die. On the district board were people of vision, among them several retired denominational leaders and pastors, who also wanted to see the district grow. They decided to make a study of the Naples area to see if it was a good place to start a church. They approached Earle Fike, the denominational executive in charge of Parish Ministries. Merle Crouse remembers, "Earle was realizing it was time to get something going again in new church development. He was waiting for an opening."

At that time, church extension work was only a small part of the denomination's program. It was only one of several large responsibilities in the job description of denominational staff member Hubert Newcomer. But like Earle, Hubert was interested in the Florida idea. He called Don Robinson, a Pennsylvania pastor with experience doing church development feasibility studies. Together, Merle, Hubert, and Don studied Lee and Collier counties in southwestern Florida.

They found that Naples in Collier County was not a good site for a new church. But up the coast forty miles, at the entrance to the Caloosahatchee River was a rapidly growing new community called Cape Coral, which looked more promising. What the district board and Merle Crouse had in mind was not a church of retired Brethren gathered together by a retired minister, an all too frequent pattern in Florida, but a vigorous new church, with a strong, aggressive pastor, in a new community where there were no Brethren.

The district board voted to go ahead with this kind of new church project; Cape Coral was chosen as the site; and Merle as district executive began the pastoral search process. Don Shank, pastor of the church in Elgin, Illinois, responded, and the district board interviewed him at the 1975 Annual Conference. Don brought several qualifications to the job. He was an experienced pastor with 13 years service in the large, diverse Elgin church. As such he was Earle's and Hubert's pastor and had been Merle's when he lived in Elgin, so he knew these three men well and they knew him. Before coming to Elgin, he had started a new church at Drexel Hill near Philadelphia, Pennsylvania, which in eight years he had built into a thriving group of 210 members. Also, Don was an outdoorsman and a jogger, who liked warm weather. Having been at the Elgin church for more than a decade, he felt it was time for a change. All factors, experience, the trust necessary for close cooperation in a risky venture, and personal considerations, seemed to come together. The district board called Don at that 1975 Conference and he accepted.

All this was new to everyone involved. Each step had to be taken carefully. One of the most important considerations was financing. The district began a venture fund to raise some of the money. General Board (the body elected by Annual Conference to oversee denominational program and employ denominational staff) agreed to a rather sizable yearly commitment, given its limited resources. An estimate was made of what the members of the new church might be expected to contribute. Hubert Newcomer, Merle Crouse, and Don Shank did some careful thinking to lay out the finances and project them over four years, but when all these sources were tallied, they still fell short of what was needed. Don Shank offered to raise the difference. He contacted friends, family, and former parishioners and received commitments of about $25,000 to be spread over the four years. The goal was to be self-supporting at the end of the fourth year.

And so in January, 1976, Don and Eileen Shank moved to Cape Coral to begin a new church, and without anyone knowing it at the time, a new church development movement was beginning as well. A pattern of local initiative, feasibility study, fiscal planning, and Brotherhood/district/local cooperation was being developed and tested which with modifications would eventually become the methodology of the movement.

Don sensed the importance of what they were doing. "I felt God had called me here," he says now. "I was challenged by the adventurousness and the excitement of starting something new, but more than that, I felt that the Church of the Brethren had no choice but to get into new church development. In the sixties our emphasis was social action. I felt very much and still do that [social action] is a necessary part of our witness, but I just felt we needed to get into church development."

So with a sense of excitement and a sense of the auspiciousness of his work, Don began to acquaint himself with Cape Coral. In March, 1976, he called together the first group of worshipers. Including Don and Eileen, they numbered twelve. "We talked about feeling the call of God to form a congregation," Don remembers. "We really did want to be open to the movement of God's Spirit. We really weren't here to do our thing but to find out what was God's thing."

What Don had in mind was a house church, a small, closely-knit fellowship of believers and seekers, meeting to worship and support one another. The group met in Don and Eileen's home and in other informal settings, sometimes even on the beach. With his experience Don thought that starting this new church would be easy. But this was not to be.

"It was really rough going the first year," Don says. "I had a vision that we would come down here and somehow this thing would just take off. And it didn't. The first thing that really took off was a sunrise service at the yacht club beach on Easter Sunday. We put a big ad in the paper. We had 96 people there sitting in the sand. I was in heaven! I thought, 'We have arrived! This is it!' We made an attempt to get everybody to sign cards and to invite them back to the yacht club right there in that area next Sunday. The next Sunday we had 13 people in worship! After that I just felt like the bottom had fallen out, and it was almost like from that Sunday on we could hardly make it through the summer. We'd have eight or ten people in worship. You know, you can't even sing with that few! We limped along and limped along."

Don and others realized the house church was not going to work at Cape Coral. People did not feel comfortable coming to a private home for worship. A more public place was needed, and so for several months the group met at the yacht club. But the church did not grow. It dragged on into its second year. It changed its meeting place to a room at First Federal Savings and Loan. Don's discouragement deepened. Virgil Hylton, present moderator of the church and one of the original twelve people, remembers that time, "Once I met him in the lobby of the bank. He had called me. We didn't even have an office then. So we just sat there in the bank lobby in a quiet place and he said, 'Virg, there's no way! No use! It's just not gonna go! It's not gonna fly!'"

"I was struggling with some personal issues," Don remembers. "Who am I and what is my life all about? Somewhere somebody had told me that we need to learn to live without God, that it's immature to be dependent upon God; and it did almost seem to me that a mature Christian is one who doesn't always need to be running to God and saying, 'I need this. I need that.' I was distancing myself from God, from the personal God, from the God I needed. It was almost like I was saying, 'I really don't need you. I can do it without you.' Here in Cape Coral it hit me profoundly, 'I can't do it alone, Lord. This is your work, and if you're not in it and a part of it and a part of me, it is not going to go! That's all there is to it!' The paradox of life is that we don't want that which is painful, but we realize when we look back over our lives that it is the pain that causes us either to grow or to regress."

Gradually Don grew. "You could almost feel the change in his approach, his message," says Bailey Hathaway, a retired Baptist minister who was one of the original twelve. "He was more positive about what God could do for people." Don's attitude toward preaching itself changed. Always the experimenter, he had been trying dialogue worship services. Now the preached word came to have more power. "There is the moment when I stand to preach. We turn the lights down, and we focus the attention on the preached word. It becomes very silent and very reverent. And I tell you, I feel the Spirit moving! Somehow that doesn't quite come across when I'm sitting down leading a Bible discussion." The change was felt in the church in another way. The congregation gave up the hope of having a church without an edifice and in 1978 started a building fund.

In an account of this sort you expect to hear that now there was a great harvest of new members; the spiritual growth brought numerical growth. But this did not happen at Cape Coral. The membership growth since then has been steady but unspectacular. In 1980, the congregation dedicated a compact, well-designed church building with movable chairs in the sanctuary, which doubles as a fellowship hall. As of the end of 1983, the church has a membership of 94 and an average attendance of 83. It has been supporting itself since 1980 and receives no funds from the district or the General Board. Don Shank is not on full salary, but on three-quarters support. In the other quarter of his time, he serves as a counselor, a kind of chaplain, for several Cape Coral banks. His contacts in this work have helped bring new members. As 1984 begins, the congregation is experiencing a growth spurt. Its small sanctuary sometimes overflows on Sunday mornings. The church in Cape Coral is a solid small church. Still it is not the sort of booming venture that church planters usually hope for or what Don Shank expected.

There are several reasons for this. One is that people come and go in Florida. Don comments that there have been three different congregations in the church's short history. Each time enough people were lost that the character of the congregation changed. Then too, because Cape Coral was the first new congregation in the district and the Brotherhood in some time, there was no clear model to follow. Everything was new. It took the congregation more than a year and a half to decide what kind of church they wanted to be. Further, slow growth is rooted in the character of the Church of the Brethren. Peter Nead, influential nineteenth century Brethren writer, quoting from 2 Timothy, warned against "leading captive silly persons." Even when converts came to the church in great ardor, elders were known to advise them to cool down and think carefully about their decision, to count the cost. Merle Crouse said recently, "Evangelism means to build up the church and not just to save individuals. The church is the proof of the pudding' on whether or not you're being effective—the faith community." Finally, the slow growth is consonant with the character of the Cape Coral church itself, the mission concept they finally settled on, and the name they chose—Christ the Servant. "The Lord was a serving Christ," Don says. "If we really wanted to be his church in this place, we needed to be a servant people, not so much in terms of size or prominence but in a low-key, very quiet, penetrating way, like salt. That's what we were going to be about."

So to find the growth at Christ the Servant Church in Cape Coral, you have to look somewhere other than at the membership roll. "This church accepts you just where you are," says Doris Galvin, who came from Ohio with a Brethren, Reformed, and Mennonite background. "I don't think it makes any difference whether you are financially low or high."

Peg Heppe, a retired school teacher with strong views on peace, who had never felt comfortable in a church until joining Christ the Servant, says, "The people are warm, caring, sharing people. Those who come for the first time feel it. It seeps into the atmosphere. The church ministers to the needs of people like me, unorthodox, not calmly accepting, and therefore not taken care of by any other church."

"The church is for people who are having problems, not for the perfect people," says Lynn Gilmore, who came from a Catholic background. "We go there to get better. I don't feel there's any pressure on me to achieve a certain point of religion, rather to intermingle religion with the rest of life." Lynn is an interior decorator with a love of beautiful things that shows in her clothes and her home. "The one problem when I first started was that one of the beliefs in the church is the simple life. My profession kind of belies that. I felt, 'Oh, gee, I don't know if they're going to like me.' But the church draws me away from that attitude where women are worrying about what color lamp they're going to put on the table. It gets me to think that there are other things in life besides money and decorating. There are some spiritual things."

"Don Shank emphasizes human frailty and how to rise above it," says Peg Heppe. "He knows what's bugging people, and he tries to bring us hope. The big thing about Don Shank is his own joy in his faith, a joy that is so contagious." And Elaine Smith, church soloist, who with her husband Bob, a retired American Baptist minister, recently joined Christ the Servant, says, "You really feel a spirit in that church. That's one of the things I find exciting, that so many Sundays you really feel the presence of God in the worship service."

Ron Gibbs, the 1983 board chairperson, was a skeptic when he came and still is in some things. Ron says, "Jesus was sent to reassure us and to show us. Without him we would not have the dedication we have. He came to shore us up, to give us something to believe in again." Don Shank says, "There isn't anybody in this congregation who isn't hurting in one way or another." Christ the Servant is a church where people who are hurting or seeking or unorthodox or skeptical are helped to believe again.

This church is many things. It is a Church of the Brethren practicing trine immersion (baptism by immersing three times) in the Caloosahatchee River and the full love feast (Brethren ordinance commemorating the last supper, including a fellowship meal, communion, and feet washing); yet it is a community church that welcomes all people and does not demand compliance on points of theology and practice. It holds strongly to the Brethren peace position yet has retired military people as active members. It calls people to a simpler life yet has well-to-do retired people in its winter membership. It emphasizes spiritual life yet does not aggressively evangelize. Merle Crouse calls it a "Florida lifestyle church," informal, as much at home on the beach as in the church building.

It has acquired a group of winter members though it did not set out to be a winter church. It has people who grew up in the Church of the Brethren and have the Brethren pedigree of aunts, uncles, grandparents, and ancestors stretching back generations in the church; and it has many people who had never heard of the Brethren.

It brings together many different kinds of people and instead of trying to convert them, it serves them and invites them into a community where they can grow, can "get better." There is a kind of patience in the Christ the Servant congregation and a kind of humility. It is not renowned, but it is special. There is much that it could be, but God has blessed what it has become. It has not quite lived up to its own expectations, but it has found, in lieu of that, something more valuable.

"If you ask, 'What's the greatest thing you've learned in all this?' " Don exclaims, "I'd say, 'Patience!' Patience to rely on the slow hand of God to do his work and not always to be in such a hurry to see the results. That puts a terrible burden on you. I think God taught me,

'Don, if you go down there thinking you're going to be a smashing success and you're going to have all kinds of acclaim coming to you, I've got another thought coming for you, Buddy! You are going to sweat and you are going to hurt and you are going to get down on your knees and you're going to say, "Lord, how long!"' It's been a humbling and heartening experience to wait on the Lord."

Like Christ the Servant, Good Shepherd Church of the Brethren in Bradenton, Florida has a pastor whose personal pilgrimage has had a positive impact on the congregation. To tell the Good Shepherd story, we have to go back to 1968 and Emmanuel Evangelical United Brethren (E.U.B.) Church in Bradenton, where Don White was called to pastor. That same year the E.U.B. denomination merged with the Methodist denomination to form the huge United Methodist Church. This brought Emmanuel church under the jurisdiction of the Methodist bishop. Don White had been close to his E.U.B. superintendent, but this Methodist bishop who replaced him had a style that chafed Don. He remembers feeling like a pawn. One of the things they disagreed on was the congregation's financial obligations to the denomination.

Emmanuel church was growing rapidly and began to make plans to build a new sanctuary. The differences between Don and the bishop came to a head when the bishop refused permission for the new building until Emmanuel met the denomination's financial expectations. Feeling blocked and frustrated, Don decided to resign and begin a new congregation, an independent, community church. This was the beginning of the Church of the Cross.

This congregation also grew rapidly, and within five years its membership was 500, and its attendance was sometimes more than 1,000 in the winter months. It had a new building which cost $300,000. At the hub of the church was Don White's leadership—his positive preaching, his evangelistic style, and his creative ideas. People were drawn to him and to the beautiful new building.

In 1975 Don resigned from Church of the Cross. The reason was his decision to seek a divorce. Ed Smith, who was a lay minister working on the church's staff, pastored the church for seventeen months, but the work was too strenuous for his health and he too resigned.

An independent congregation does not have the pool of ministers to draw upon or the pastoral search channels that a congregation in a denomination has. The Church of the Cross had to catch-as-catch-can to find a new pastor. According to Ray Baldridge, then moderator of the church, the man they called alienated many members almost at once. He brought with him a following of 35 people, which quickly swelled to 200. Finding this new pastor so different from the way he had presented himself in interviews, some of the leaders of the church hired a private detective, who discovered that he had misrepresented his qualifications.

Meanwhile, he was consolidating his power. The leaders went to court to stop him. The judge ruled that a congregational vote must decide if the new minister could continue. Ray remembers that this was happening during the summer months when many members were up north or traveling. Other members were leaving in dismay. And the new man was bringing in more of his own supporters. The church leaders lost the vote. They briefly considered further legal action and were advised that because the vote had gone against them they had little chance of winning a court case. So they and the former nucleus of the congregation withdrew from the church. This all happened in a matter of only three and a half months.

This disheartened and angry remnant began to meet in the Baldridge home. Ray, the moderator, and his wife Rosemary were determined to hold the group together. One Saturday night in 1976, Ray was sitting in their kitchen reading the Bible. It was late, 2:00 a.m., and he was sitting up because he could not sleep. "I don't recall what I was reading," Ray says, "but it was so true to what we were suffering through. It just hit me. I've heard people say this and I didn't believe it, but a voice from somewhere inside me, or whatever it was, said, 'Call Don White.' Out loud I said, 'Do what?' 'Call Don White.'"

Meanwhile, Don's path had not been easy either. Just as there is no established way for an independent church to find a pastor, there is no procedure for an independent pastor to find a church. For this reason and because of his divorce, which made him unacceptable to some congregations, Don did not know where to turn. After such a successful ministry, it was painful to be down and out, wondering if anyone would have him. While Don was visiting friends in Frederick, Maryland, he met Merlin Garber, who was then pastor of the Frederick Church of the Brethren. This was not Don's first contact with the Brethren. In fact, one of the persons responsible for his conversion when he was a young man in Tennessee was a young Brethren man who was attending the E.U.B. church because the Church of the Brethren in that community did not have a youth group. Merlin encouraged Don to contact Don Rowe, the Mid-Atlantic district executive, and to circulate his resumé among the Brethren. Truman Northup, the district executive for the Pacific Southwest Conference, offered Don a position as pastor of the Cajon Valley Church of the Brethren in El Cajón, California. This is where Don was serving when Ray Baldridge called him.

It was not easy for Ray to do this. Don's divorce and resignation had broken their close friendship. Ray did not even know where Don was. He did know he was somewhere in the San Diego area. He called information and to his surprise found the number. With the time difference it was 10:00 p.m., late but still early enough to call. "We hadn't talked in two or three years," Ray recalls. "He was as surprised as I was. I told him we needed help. Our first conversation was cold."

But Don called back the next night and agreed to come and talk to the group if they voted unanimously to have him. They did and they offered to pay his expenses. Don had remarried and they paid his wife Becky's expenses too. Becky's presence was important, not only because she was Don's wife but because with her musical gifts she and Don had begun to work together as a ministerial team. The understanding was that Don and Becky would come for two weeks and would help the group decide what to do. This was in January of 1977.

The first thing they did with Don's help was to plan and advertise a Sunday morning service in the auditorium of a local Christian school. Their object was to test the waters, to see whether there was interest in the kind of congregation the Church of the Cross remnant wanted. Over 200 people came that morning. The next Sunday there was another crowd of over 200. At the end of the two weeks, the group felt there was potential for a new church. They asked Don to be the pastor.

Don and Becky went back to California. They talked the call over; they prayed about it. In two weeks they made their decision. Don resigned at Cajón Valley. In April they moved to Bradenton. The group that called Don had approximately 60 active members. Calling him represented a huge financial commitment for so small a group and a risk for Don and Becky. There were moving costs, a pastoral salary, and $50 per Sunday to rent a meeting hall; and the group was still paying legal fees left over from the court fight.

They started out at the American Legion Hall, the only meeting place they could find. Each Sunday they went early and took down the bingo tables and covered up the gambling equipment. "We opened up the building so some of the cigarette, whiskey, and beer odors from the night before could get out," Don says. "I remember every Sunday looking over at the clock on the wall, which had 'Schlitz Beer' printed on it. After the service we had to take chairs down and put tables back because the bingo and drinking crowd was coming in at three." After about six months of this, they finally found the old Jones Auditorium in downtown Bradenton. This became their home for the next two and a half years.

"This church was born a full-grown church," Don says. Attendance continued to be strong. The name Church of the Good Shepherd was chosen to symbolize the style of the pastor and congregation. Don White was skillfully building another church. But this time there were differences. One of them was that Don now had a church home, the Church of the Brethren. He had joined the Brethren, and his ordination had been accepted. He had decided he would never again be an independent pastor and urged the congregation to affiliate with a denomination. He said that he would serve for a year while they were making up their mind whether and with whom to affiliate. If the decision were not to affiliate with the Brethren, he would honor his Brethren ordination and resign. The members of the congregation, still hurting from losing their church because it had no denominational connection to protect it, were willing to consider affiliation.

Don called Merle Crouse, the Florida/Puerto Rico district executive, and a meeting was set up in Lakeland, Florida for Don and Becky White and Ray and Rosemary Baldridge to meet with Merle and Jean Crouse. Ray Baldridge remembers that meeting, "I don't think anybody tasted their dinner. Then we went into the nitty-gritty—what had transpired after Don left, what prompted him to leave—all kinds of questions. Nobody tried to conceal anything. Everything was put on the table. Let the chips fall where they may. It was not easy. Not for Don, not for me, not for Merle. The ladies didn't say much."

Merle liked what he saw and heard. In fact he had seen Don's resumé as it had circulated and had noted his qualifications in new church development. He recommended to the district board that an exploration committee be named. The district and the new church agreed, as Merle describes it, "to enter a period of visiting and exploration to see if there was enough commonality for them to feel good within the Brethren with all our peculiarities and for us to feel good with them."

Merle took the lead in this process. His first visit made a good impression on the Good Shepherd people. They liked him and his calm, cool, patient manner. "A group of our people went over to Sebring [the largest Church of the Brethren in Florida]," Don remembers, "and a group of their people came over here. It was just like people dating, you know. The district responded with such love and acceptance."

But the district moved carefully. As with Cape Coral, they had no precedent. As far as Merle knew, the Church of the Brethren had never before adopted a congregation. No one knew how to do it. Ray Baldridge says, "The process was well thought out. It was studied in every direction. Merle Crouse turned over every stone he could find. It was as if he were looking for an excuse not to accept us. He had a job to do and he did it well."

There were two sticking points. One was secret societies. Some of the members at Good Shepherd were Masons. The Brethren oppose membership in secret societies. The other was the Brethren peace stand. A meeting was held in the community building of a Bradenton mobile home court where the Good Shepherd people put some frank questions. Ray Baldridge was afraid they were going to "upset the apple cart." Merle says, "There was a lot of distance for some people, but others were quite close to us." Merle clearly stated the Church of the Brethren positions and explained that the church respects differences of opinion and freedom of conscience on doctrine and practice. His answers satisfied the people who were concerned. Some of the Good Shepherd people were from the original Emmanuel Evangelical United Brethren church Don had first pastored. Some similarities between that tradition and the Church of the Brethren and the very name were positive factors.

Though there were differences, the district board and the Good Shepherd people accepted what they found in each other. In August of 1977, the board recommended that Good Shepherd be received into the district as a full-fledged congregation. In October at district conference, at the same time Cape Coral was admitted as a fellowship [an intermediate step before becoming a congregation], Good Shepherd was accepted as a congregation. A circle was formed and both new churches were given a warm welcome. "It was very meaningful for this multitude of people from so many diverse backgrounds," Don White says. Good Shepherd had a home and the District of Florida and Puerto Rico had an active new congregation.

The new church was admitted with 103 members and an average

attendance in the winter months of double that figure, and it continued to grow. Ray Baldridge observes another difference from Don White's earlier churches, "It's not growing in leaps and bounds like the Church of the Cross. It's steady, solid growth. At the Church of the Cross, the majority of the congregation worshiped the building and the man. That is not the case here." Ray, who until recently was the moderator, also talks about the changes in himself, "I try to keep a low profile. At the other church, I had too many duties, was too vocal, too much in the spotlight. I'm not going to let that happen again." And of the change in Don, he says, "He's a much better, deeper, more dedicated person now than I've ever seen him. This is the reason this congregation is growing—his deep dedication."

The transition from independent church to Brethren congregation has been gradual. At first only a few of the people meeting in Jones Auditorium came from other Brethren churches and knew what a Church of the Brethren was like. Among those few were Preston and Dorothy Gregory from the North Webster congregation in Indiana, who started meeting with the new church way back in the American Legion Hall. They were enthusiastic supporters and were afraid the Brethren in the district might not accept Good Shepherd. "The fear was that he [Don White] had such a following," Dorothy says. "You get 150-200 people following a man in the Church of the Brethren—that is very unusual. I think they were a little leery of what this was all about, whether it was a cult or what in the world it was."

"You don't feel strange in that church anymore if you're a traditional Brethren," Merle Crouse remarks. "It used to feel like a Presbyterian church, more like a mainline, downtown church. Now it has a community church feel. There are people of various backgrounds. There is no pressure to accept everything Brethren believe, but this is unapologetically presented. The church is very active in district and national church life." Don White has served as district board chairperson. Two members have entered Brethren Volunteer Service. The congregation does not stress peace as much as some congregations, but Don does not hedge on the peace stand. Good Shepherd has lost at least one member who did not want to be associated with a peace church.

It is not necessary to show how "Brethren" a church is to validate its faith and witness. Still, Brethren have deep convictions and cultural peculiarities. How does a congregation with different roots come to terms with these and how do Brethren accept adopted brothers and sisters? Observe the introduction of the love feast at Good Shepherd.

As long as the Bradenton Brethren met in the Jones Auditorium, they did not practice the love feast, but in 1980 at Easter, just after dedicating their new building, they decided it was time to begin. They turned for instruction to Preston and Dorothy Gregory, who were deacons in their home church in Indiana. The Gregorys invited 16 people over to their mobile home. "You've got to understand," says Preston. "Here we have a congregation of Presbyterians, Methodists, Baptists, Lutherans, Catholics. And you take a pastor who's trying to encourage a love feast. And the people are older—hard to change.

"Now, here that night," Preston goes on, "the women were out there [kitchen]; the men in here [living room]. At first one of my buddies said nobody's going to wash his feet. But we didn't leave anything out. We had everything just like we have it up north. We didn't know whether they would ever do it again. I gave them a little talk and I said, 'Now this might be as close as you'll ever get to your Lord. It all depends on you. If you will look at it the right way and worship and follow the scripture that our pastor is going to read and do these things, I think you'll like it.' Then we went through it. My buddy washed my feet. I washed his. They were so impressed with it they decided to go with it. At the first love feast [in the church], I actually saw young men cry."

Close to 90 people participated in that first love feast. The service continues to be attended by only a portion of the congregation, but those from other traditions who experience it for the first time almost to a person testify to its meaning for them. One of the ironies is that often among those who do not participate are Brethren from up north who grew up with the practice.

Don White stimulates people, gets them interested. Something is always happening at Good Shepherd. Very early they bought a lot and started their building program. People pitched in to clear away brush and volunteered to put up paneling and paint the interior. Arthur Dean, retired Brethren architect, donated the design of the building. The striking exterior juts out into a lake in front of it like the prow of a ship. Inside it is decorated in attractive earth tones. There is a stained glass image of Christ as the Good Shepherd above the chancel. The congregation used the fund-raising process to stir up interest and get people involved. Contributors purchased windows and bought benches. Members can point to things they either made or bought and feel a part of the building. Already, in 1983, an extension was added to each of the wings.

There is no yearly stewardship campaign or pledging process. The budget is published each year so people know what the church will need and tithing is encouraged. Then there are regular fundraising emphases during the year. One is called Save Our Summer (SOS). Each spring just before the winter residents go north, Don asks for a special offering to get the church through the summer period of diminished attendance and giving. Then in the dead of summer, the month of August, the bane of south Florida churches, Good Shepherd runs an enthusiastic fund drive called the Summer Slump Jump. The drive is designed so that the goal is always reached. There is a deliberate attempt to increase attendance. New members are taken in. So in the worst doldrums of summer, people at Good Shepherd have a church that is alive, not languishing; people up north for the summer read the newsletter, see what they are missing, and want to get back; and in the process money is raised. In addition to the regular emphases, Good Shepherd often raises money spontaneously. When the congregation learned that Bob and Martie Kaufman, BVSers on Culebra, an island off the coast of Puerto Rico, needed a four-wheel drive vehicle, they got together and in a week's time raised the money.

Since Good Shepherd has moved into its building, more and more Brethren, first from Indiana, then Ohio, and now Pennsylvania are making it their winter church home. There have been enough members from Indiana that for the past four years, each summer after Annual Conference, the Gregorys have held an "Indiana Rally" for Good Shepherd people back in their home state for the summer. Don and Becky, on their way back from Conference, have been the honored guests. In 1983, rallies were also held in Ohio and Pennsylvania. Attendance at these three events in 1983 was 150 people.

Good Shepherd has a strong music program which Becky White directs. Though she is not hired as a full-time minister of music, in effect that is what she is. The music has a gospel beat and features a 40-member choir lead by Becky. Several times a year there is a Sunday afternoon Music Hall, where the members of the congregation are invited to share their talents. Good Shepherd also has a strong hospital ministry, and Don has worked consciously at ministering to retired persons.

Having so many elderly people who are willing to work and have time to give has been one of the strengths of this church. But it has also meant that until recently there have been very few young families and middle-aged people. The children's Sunday school was very small, and people with children were reluctant to join. That is slowly changing. There is now an adult group called the "Inbetweens," made up of people who are not retired, and the children's Sunday school has grown to 40 participants.

The mix of people from many traditions and traditional Brethren (or new Brethren and old Brethren as they call one another), of pastor as promoter and pastor as shepherd, of evangelicalism and peace, of aggressive, enthusiastic fund-raising and warm, caring fellowship, of churchly formality and down-home informality make this an unusual Church of the Brethren.

It is also a very successful church. Of the new congregations, it started out with the largest nucleus and remains the largest in membership and attendance. Don White is a pastor accustomed to success. But people, especially those who have been in the church since the beginning and were members of the Church of the Cross, remember that it was born out of bitter failure for them and personal anguish for Don. "The church here is a hospital for sinners," Don says, "and we all identify with each other in our brokenness, our faults, our failures. Maybe one of the reasons why we grow is that in the main the leadership of the church, including the pastor, is not bent on getting everybody straightened out. We feel that people may come with all their imperfections and all their sin and share in the life of this church. When they come here, we say to them, 'We love you and we understand. We accept you. Can we walk with you from where you are now?'" This spirit protects them against the real temptation to be big and successful for success' sake.

Lurking in the background of new church development in the seventies and eighties is the new church movement of the fifties and sixties. Over and over that work is remembered, usually for its mistakes. New work is often guided by conscious efforts to avoid those mistakes. The view most people take is that the earlier movement died out and there was a ten- to twelve-year hiatus before new churches were again started.

In the District of Northern Ohio, the Brethren do not take that view. It is true that between 1955 and 1962 they started four new churches and that between 1962 and 1977 they did not start any, but they were not inactive. "Through those years the church extension commission was involved in giving supervision to the four churches we had started and in trying to bail ourselves out of the tremendous debt we had gotten into," Gordon Bucher, the district executive, says. "It took us a decade to get that accomplished, and then we began to make some plans for new church development. When we did start, we didn't realize that there was going to be a flurry of church extension in the Brotherhood. We were just ready to start a new church, and so we went about that process." There was no dramatic turnaround, just a steady adherence to course. That description might be used for the church they started.

On August 17, 1974, the Northern Ohio district conference adopted as one of its five-year goals the establishment of a new church. In November of that year, the district church extension commission met with George Schreckengost from the Northeast Ohio Church Planning Association. The commission also met in separate sessions with representatives from churches in the western and eastern halves of the district. In February of 1975, they called Hubert Newcomer at the church headquarters in Elgin to inquire about Brotherhood support. In April, Hubert flew to Ohio and met with the commission. He recommended more study and suggested they contact Don Robinson. Based on Don's feasibility study, the commission at its June meeting prepared a recommendation to the district board "that we proceed with plans for the formation and establishment of a new congregation in Jackson Township, Stark County." The recommendation passed at district board meeting on November 15.

During the first half of 1976, the commission worked on funding, buying a lot, and finding a pastor. A funding scheme was approved with contributions from the district, the General Board, the new church itself through offerings, and individuals and congregations of the district. Several lots were considered, and in 1976 five acres were purchased on Wales Road, a main north/south route. The district paid $25,000 cash for the property, using money from the sale of a church that had closed. In April, the commission called Herb Fisher to be pastor, and Herb and his wife Helen accepted. The Fishers moved from Ivy Farms Church of the Brethren, Newport News, Virginia, in late December, and on January 1, 1977, they began their work.

Jackson Township is a growing area on the edge of Massillon, an old industrial city of 30,557. Over its rolling hills are scattered new subdivisions, sprawling shopping centers, crowded arteries, and new expressways, interspersed with farms left over from earlier days.

Demography showed this would be a good place to start a church.

Herb lost no time getting started. He is a dogged worker. Merle Crouse has said that of all the pastor/developers, Herb has worked the most consistently over the years at knocking on doors. Larry Bradley, professor of education at the University of Akron, remembers that Herb knocked on his door just after he had gotten off an airline flight that had been so turbulent that two nuns sitting near him had been saying their rosary. "You came at the right time!" he exclaimed. The Bradleys sent Herb down the street to the Byrds who were also interested. By mid-March, Herb had gathered enough interested people that he was ready to move to the next step. On Sunday evening, March 13, 1977, at the parsonage on Mudbrook Street, the Jackson Township Fellowship met for the first time. Twenty-five people came.

Very quickly the group found the parsonage inadequate, and arrangements were made to meet across the street in the gymnasium of the Jackson Memorial Middle School. This became their home for the next three and a half years. Each Sunday they carried chairs, hymnbooks, and banners from the Fishers' garage, set up for worship, and then carried everything back.

It was the district's plan and Herb's intention to build a church of people who did not have Brethren background. In earlier developments the district had had its fill of trying to gather scattered Brethren and did not believe this was a good way to start a church. Of those first 25 people, only Herb and Helen were members of the Church of the Brethren. As Gordon Bucher describes it, Herb "won that church out of the community." "My wife and I were raised Methodist, attended a Presbyterian college, joined the United Church of Christ, and then joined the Church of the Brethren," Larry Bradley remarks. As the group grew, people came from Catholic, Anglican, and Baptist backgrounds as well as others. There were even some from the Church of the Brethren eventually.

Herb slowly introduced Brethren ideas and practices, carefully explaining them. He handled the love feast very carefully, Larry remembers. When the peace position was explained, one family with a military background dropped out (though they remained friends with Herb). But there was never the feeling that the Brethren way was a condition of acceptance. On the contrary, people's ideas were welcomed. Dale Garver, who had a Brethren background but had lived in Kentucky and attended other churches for many years and who joined the group late in 1978, says of the variety of backgrounds, "I think it's good because it doesn't let us get too lazy in our thinking. There are a lot of folks who can share attitudes from their experiences that are unique. Had we all been Brethren by tradition, we might not have been as broad."

What was it that attracted these people? "We liked Herb," says Dorothy Bradley. "He came across as a very human, caring kind of individual." "We liked the church," Larry adds, "because the church is basically like that. It puts its money where its mouth is. It gets actively involved. It's really unique. We've just really enjoyed it. It just has a lot of meaning to it. It's like a family. I don't know, in talking to other people, any church quite like it. There's just something unique about the Brethren church. When you go to meetings—district conference, for instance—it's just there, a feeling that you have. People really do care. It's too bad that more people don't know about that.

"It's part of their heritage apparently," Larry goes on. "It's part of what they believe. That's what Christ taught. Love. They really try to practice that. It's not an abstract thing. It's a real thing. It's a quality I think is very rare. I don't know of any other church that we've ever been associated with that I could actually say that that's true."

The new fellowship elected a steering committee and began to organize itself. Larry Bradley was elected chairman. A name was chosen: Trinity Church of the Brethren. In August, 1978, district conference gave Trinity fellowship status. Attendance statistics show steady growth. By mid-1979, Trinity was averaging more than 60 people a Sunday.

All this time the members were carrying all the paraphernalia of worship across the street to the middle school in a pickup truck. They were tired of doing this. It was time, they felt, to start talking about a building. In every other new congregation that has completed its building, there is a nostalgia for the old days in the bank building or the auditorium or the fire hall, but at Trinity there is no such feeling. They were fed up with the high ceiling, bad acoustics, impersonal atmosphere, inadequate Sunday school rooms, and hard work that went with meeting in the gym. They were ready to build.

One of the things that attracted Dale and Nancy Garver to the church was that it already had a building lot. Dale, Senior EDP Auditor for Firestone Tire and Rubber Company, saw the lot and the full-time pastor as a sign that the Ohio Brethren meant business at Trinity. He thought with that backing they could take the next step. He felt the families had all the gifts to make the church happen. It became evident when they started to ask who can do what that they had a unique mixture. For Dale and Nancy it was more than unique. It was providential. "When we moved here," Nancy says, "we did not look around as much as we have done before. We prayed about it and felt perhaps this was where the Lord wanted us."

The Trinity folks began to confer with Arthur Dean, the retired Church of the Brethren architect who was then also designing the buildings for Christ the Servant and Good Shepherd. As they prepared themselves for the building program, they experienced their first setback. Several families pulled out of the church. No one quite knows why. One story is that the financial commitment looked too big. Another story is that one of the people clashed with Herb. A third reading is that one of the families who had been in the inner circle since the first meeting could not gracefully share the leadership as the church grew.

Herb recalls that time, "I remember sitting down with the steering committee and just saying, 'What do you make of this? It's discouraging. I feel it. I'm sure you do. What do you make of it?' Here's where the old Southern Baptist gal, Bev Byrd, said, 'Well, if it's the Lord's work, it'll go anyway.' Every once in a while, you just have to pull yourself up short and say who you're working for. She was a good one to do that." It was not long after, however, that the Byrds had to leave too, transferred to Oklahoma.

But Trinity survived these losses and went on with their plans. In April of 1980, they broke ground. They arranged to have Maurice Snyder, a retired contractor from the First Church of the Brethren in Canton, and his son Edison supervise the job. A mason from the Paradise congregation volunteered the brick work. Herb estimates close to six thousand hours of volunteer labor went into the church. To put the roof on, the district called a work day. Larry Bradley recalls that it was like an Amish barn-raising. Women got up on the roof and helped right along with the men. The building was built for only $184,000, and the group effort that saved the money also brought the church together.

"I really think the Lord wanted this church here," Dale Garver says. "I look back now and I know we were watched over. No one got hurt. Hardly anything went wrong. It was done in less than a year. We had novices working in places where they could get hurt."

In November, 1980, the Trinity people heaved a sigh of relief and moved into their new building. It was still unfinished, but to them it was wonderful. Don Battershell, looking back now, says they went too fast. He feels they burned themselves out. They were so tired of the gym that they knocked themselves out to do the work. He feels the program went flat for a while after they moved in.

The building showed the community that Trinity was there to stay and enabled the church to reach out. "I started out working on the idea that when we get a building, it's to be used, not looked at," says Herb. "It's not our building. It's a building dedicated to the work of the Lord and to the community and to our neighbor's good." Trinity opened its doors to scout groups, to the American Association of Retired Persons, and to other community organizations.

Still, the church building was not finished. Finally, in early 1983, with the help of grants from the General Board and the district, the congregation bought pews and a fellowship hall divider, finished the kitchen and classrooms, and had the property landscaped. Its pews are unique because they are not fastened down and can be placed in any configuration or removed for fellowship activities.

Today Trinity has a membership of 109. It has a mix of ages and vocations, as well as backgrounds. Many of its members work in middle-management in businesses and other organizations. It is a suburban, community-minded church with a Brethren identity and an open attitude. Its growth is steady but slow. "I'm not concerned about size primarily," Herb Fisher says. "I'm concerned about quality and what happens to people. I don't see that it's going to mushroom. I hope it will have a good, steady growth over the years. The thrust of the kingdom is always to go where people are, go into the world, and proclaim the gospel. It's the mission of the church to get out and find people and get them involved in the kingdom. That's why I'm here."

Church development consultants often observe how much a new church reflects the leadership style of its pastor. Herb Fisher is not dramatic, but he gets the job done. He's not afraid to take risks. He is reflective and articulate. He is liberal in theology and believes in a community-oriented church. This characterization could describe Trinity. But Herb also has a kind of bulldog individuality that sometimes sets him over against his congregation. He is not afraid to disagree, and people at Trinity are not afraid to disagree. This releases the Trinity members from the emotional dependence that some churches have on their founding pastor.

Larry Bradley, who has been with Trinity since the beginning and who was on the early steering committee and was the first chairperson of the board is a professor of education and thinks of himself as an objective social scientist. He offers some observations on what a new church needs. "You've got to have good pastoral leadership. I would say don't be afraid to try. Don't be afraid to make decisions without knowing all the facts. If you wait until all the facts are in, you're never going to get anything done. And you've got to have —and it's true; I didn't believe it, but now I know it's true—you've got to have trust in God and have faith it will happen. And it will! You don't have to know everything. You learn as you develop. You will be surprised. People will come along. We've had it happen. Someone will say, 'Well, here's a thousand dollars we'd like for you to have.' It does happen." Here is an objective social scientist saying you can rely on the grace of God. "That's right," Larry says. "You can!"

By various estimates, the idea of starting a church in the vicinity of Lampeter in Lancaster County, Pennsylvania, goes back 15 years and maybe as many as 30 years. In this county, thickly populated with Churches of the Brethren, there was a gap between the Lancaster congregation on the north and Mechanic Grove on the south. But the talk of putting a church in this area always died out or was discouraged, and nothing was ever done. Then when the talk did finally turn to action, it came from an unexpected source.

In 1974 a group of members of the Mechanic Grove congregation wanted to make it a charismatic church. Mechanic Grove is a large, strong, rural church in the southern part of the county. Like many Brethren churches in those parts, it had a good program, a good pastor, and good fellowship and was pretty comfortable with itself. This charismatic challenge really upset its members. Clarence Wenger, who owns a tire business in Lancaster, remembers, "I had *The Fruits of the Spirit* in one hand and was buffing tires with the other because I had nobody to give me any answers, and I was the church board chairman." Earl Ziegler, who was the pastor, says, "The charismatic movement made us get down on our knees, but better than that it made our leaders study their Bibles. The charismatics knew their scripture!"

In November of that year the board decided it was time to face the issue and to face it head on. They brought a resolution to the congregational business meeting that "the church members and/or persons who worship at the Mechanic Grove Church of the Brethren support our pastor and the ministry of the Mechanic Grove Church of the

Brethren." The resolution went on to call members and worshipers to "avoid a critical attitude" and to support the church with both prayer and attendance and concluded by stating that anyone not able to accept the leadership and authority of the pastor as guided by the church board "shall seek a church home where his spiritual needs can be met." The resolution passed by a vote of 128 to 14. It reaffirmed the church's direction and isolated the dissenters, twelve of whom eventually left the church.

The other major item on the agenda that night was the church building. The congregation was growing and needed more space; it was time to build an addition and to enlarge the sanctuary. In the middle of that discussion, Sadie Kreider stood up and said, as Earl Ziegler remembers it, "If we find our faith so meaningful, maybe we ought to share it and not keep it to ourselves. Why don't we consider starting a new church instead of building bigger?"

Sadie is a quiet lady who still dresses "plain" and wears the prayer covering. (Plain, unadorned clothing was once worn by all Brethren, and the women wore a lace head covering.) She has a generous, liberal spirit, and she believes that change and growth are opportunities, not threats. "I felt we ought to reach out," Sadie says, looking back. "We're so satisfied. We are! I am! I have a feeling that I ought to do more than I'm doing. That's the way I felt."

Earl recalls that Sadie sat down and said no more after her one short speech, but the idea dropped into receptive minds. There was very little more said about building. By the end of the meeting, a motion was made and passed "that we look into starting another church somewhere instead of enlarging the present building." A committee was appointed for that task. That action was the beginning of what eventually became the Lampeter Church of the Brethren.

Clarence Wenger believes the two actions at that meeting were related. "The problem we had was the first step that was necessary before starting the new church," he says. "It was the greatest thing that ever happened to the Mechanic Grove church. It made people take a stand. I think it was a little bit like the grain of sand in the oyster; it irritated and the pearl was formed around it."

Over the next three years, things moved slowly. There were meetings with Harold Bomberger, the Atlantic Northeast district executive, who was open to the project. There was a meeting at Gap, Pennsylvania, to consider starting the church in that area. In May of 1976, the district invited representatives from the area Churches of the Brethren to discuss the idea. There was interest and the district witness commission asked Don Robinson to do a feasibility study. His report, completed in December of that year, showed that the Willow Street/Lampeter area was a more likely site than Gap. It was the second fastest growing section of the county. In May of 1977, the Mechanic Grove congregational business meeting asked the Atlantic Northeast district witness commission to contact persons interested in forming a fellowship in the Willow Street area. The district and Mechanic Grove together called a meeting of interested people in July at the home of Carl and Anna Mae Diller, Mechanic Grove members living in the Lampeter area. Eighteen people attended.

In 1977, Jeff Rutt, Sadie Kreider's grandson, who was only 19 years old at the time, became chairperson of the Mechanic Grove witness commission. He began to push. He remembers that the project seemed to be floundering. It seemed to need "something to get it over the edge." On November 1, the witness commission sent a motion to the church board recommending that a Bible study be held in 1978 in the Lampeter area during Lent and that worship services begin on the first Sunday in April. Jeff remembers that the motion was a shock to the board at its November 14 meeting. People did not think it would work. Clarence Wenger, the board chairperson, opposed the idea. (Later he changed his mind and enthusiastically supported it.) But the motion passed the congregational business meeting on November 16; the vote was 50 to 24. "I felt it was God's will," Jeff says. "I had no doubts about that. It's hard to explain. It just seemed like everything added up."

The Bible study group, led by Vivian Ziegler, Earl's wife, began meeting in February. A committee of three began looking for a place to hold worship. The district prepared a letter inviting interested people to the first worship service. But the three men who were looking for a meeting place could not find one. They really wanted the Lampeter Fire Hall, but they were refused permission to use it because two other religious groups had recently been turned down. The men continued to search and the Bible study group prayed about the matter. One night while they were meeting at the Dillers, the phone rang. It was the fire hall representatives. The three men quickly went over to the hall and were told yes the fire hall could be rented. The spokesman said, "We know the Brethren. They do not steal sheep, and they are community-minded and will do much good in our community." Promptly, the prepared letter was sent from the district office, and on April 2, 1978, the Lampeter fellowship gathered for their first worship.

"Early that morning I stood on the top step and waited," remembers Earl Ziegler, who was to lead the worship and preach. "I had to say, 'Lord, you're in charge.' I was overly elated at the potential. At the same time I was scared that our dreams were overly ambitious and foolhardy. And then one car, two cars, a couple walking, a truck full of kids—a new church was born!" Forty-two people attended that morning. Twenty-three came from Mechanic Grove. Five came from other Churches of the Brethren. Five came from other religious backgrounds. And nine were visitors. Twenty-five of those people are still active six years later.

The Lampeter story is one of almost unbroken progress. Earl Ziegler filled the pulpit those first two months. After the 9:00 service at Lampeter, he would quickly drive the 10 miles to Mechanic Grove and preach again. The Mechanic Grove board voted to cover any expenses that the new fellowship could not handle, but Lampeter got off to such a good start that they never had to ask. Mechanic Grove freed Earl from some of his duties and also voted to give Lampeter regular financial support.

In June 1978, Tim Jones, a United Church of Christ student at Princeton Theological Seminary became the Lampeter summer pastor. His wife, Jill Zook Jones, also a Princeton student, was serving as summer intern at Mechanic Grove. The district gave $300 per month toward his support. "Tim came and he cared," says Bonny Frick, Lampeter church historian. "He made it his job to get out and find people. His sermons were good. His worship services were well planned. He was good for us." "He was a rookie, but a hardworking rookie," her husband Bob says. "His first sermon was 'Grasshoppers in the Land of Giants.' That was thematic of what he was doing and what Lampeter was doing."

When Tim and Jill returned to Princeton in September, Earl Ziegler resumed the pastoral duties. On October 14, district conference voted fellowship status for Lampeter. At the fellowship's congregational business meeting on November 30, Earl Kurtz, retired treasurer of Elizabethtown College, was called to be part-time pastor. And on December 31, the new church held its Charter Day. One hundred sixteen worshipers gathered in the fire hall. Earl Ziegler and Earl Kurtz led the celebration to symbolize the mother church and the daughter fellowship. Forty-nine charter members were received; 17

came from Mechanic Grove; 4 came from each of the Conestoga and Lancaster congregations; 7 came from 5 other Churches of the Brethren; and the rest came from United Church of Christ, Church of God, Quaker, Methodist, Catholic, and Jewish backgrounds. Nine of the 49 were baptized; the rest were received by a transfer of membership or a reaffirmation of faith.

Tim Jones came back from Princeton and announced that he had decided to enter the Brethren ministry. Though he could have come in on his former baptism, he elected to be rebaptized, and then he remained in the water and baptized Tim and Jean Brown, two of the new members. Then there was a surprise. Mechanic Grove presented Bob Frick, the Lampeter board chairperson, with a check for $7,600. The presentation was made by Sadie Kreider, whose vision four years earlier had made the new church possible. It was announced that the average attendance for the nine months of 1978 was 68 and the average weekly giving was $275.78.

During that first year, members of the fellowship began to look around for property. They had their eye on a piece of land on Lampeter Road at the edge of town, but the owner would not sell. They were temporarily stymied. Then one evening, as Earl Ziegler remembers it, Harlan Keener, a member of the building committee, was walking from his house to his barn. Suddenly he had an inspiration to go talk to the Herrs who owned a florist business across the road from the property they were interested in. When he went to see them, Mrs. Herr said, "Harlan, you wouldn't be here to look for land for a church, would you? I had a dream that this is a place for a church." The Herrs sold six acres to the new church at a low price. Earl Ziegler gets tears in his eyes when he talks about the Herrs. "That's such strong evidence!" he says. "How can you fight that? Every time we got to a place where we needed something, the doors opened."

Earl Kurtz served as pastor from December to May, 1979, and then for the summer months Ken Hartman, a career counselor and minister from the Lancaster congregation, took the pastoral responsibilities. In October, Earl Kurtz agreed to a second part-time stint.

In 1979 the congregation began to work seriously on plans for a building, and Earl Kurtz was the right person for that time. He took the building program as his personal ministry, letting the strong lay leadership carry responsibilities for witness and nurture, as they had already been doing. His special skills were in finance and facility planning. But he did not neglect worship. "Outside the church setting,"

Bob Frick remembers, "you saw him as the finance man. There was an altogether different personality when he stood behind that pulpit. He would start to glow." Bonnie Frick adds, "His eyes would twinkle. He was almost like a little Santa Claus. He was an interim, part-time pastor who drew people! Many people came because of him. In his sermons, he didn't look at a note. I always say he's like Will Rogers. A little guy who leans on the pulpit and just talks, and you listen."

Earl Kurtz had several goals. He was determined the fellowship would build a building that fit their real needs, not their imagined ones; and he wanted to make sure they did not get themselves stuck with a huge debt. He and Bob Frick, an elementary school principal with a penchant for administration, went to work on the second problem first. Up to this point, the Atlantic Northeast district had cooperated with and endorsed everything that had happened. Harold Bomberger, district executive, and David Markey, associate district executive, were fully involved in all decisions. The district had provided some funding. Letters about the effort had come out of the district office. Earl Ziegler and Mechanic Grove had been careful to see that things followed proper channels. But Mechanic Grove was the real impetus behind Lampeter. The district board was able to take a wait-and-see attitude. Now it was time, Bob Frick and Earl Kurtz thought, for the district to support the project more actively by helping with the building program. Earl began to talk to members of the district board. His years at the college and his contacts in the district were a great help. But what the district would do could not be known. On September 24, 1979, the Lampeter people went to district board meeting to make their request for money. Bob Frick remembers that until that night he was never sure the district was fully behind Lampeter. Bob, who came from a Church of God background, describes that meeting.

"I'd never been to district board meeting. An overwhelming feeling was how sour and serious everyone looked as I looked around the table. We were on the other side, and we were to give a progress report on what we were doing. They were talking back and forth and asking questions. 'Well, have you done this? Have you done that? Why don't you do this next?' And everything that was being suggested had been done like three months before. We had passed that point! I don't know if they were frustrated with our speed or overwhelmed by our speed or unbelieving of our speed or whatever. But it almost seemed like a 'them-and-us' meeting, the Lampeter folks versus the district board; until suddenly out of the clear blue sky, Ray Kurtz [a district board member] made the motion that they fund Lampeter for a building. We all just sat there! And if we'd all had dentures, I'm sure they'd have been on the floor! Just one of those amazing times! Still as I look back, I can't figure out where in the world that came from. It was an adversary relationship and suddenly—Boom! We're partners! It was like the board was saying, 'Now hold on. We're the district board. You're a new fellowship. Take your time. The world's young yet.' And our people were basically saying, 'Come on, come on, come on! Let's get going!' We really chomped at the bit."

What was even more astonishing was that the district board voted to pay 80 percent of the building costs up to $400,000. (Included in this figure was the anticipated General Board grant of $25,000.) Even Earl Kurtz, who had an inkling the district would do something, was amazed. "I almost fell out of my chair! It passed!"

Earl Kurtz's other concern was that the new fellowship not follow stereotyped ideas about what a church building should be. He particularly wanted to see more creative use of the sanctuary space. The building committee came to share his vision. In fact, they dropped their first architect because he was not willing to be creative. The building they eventually decided upon has a high, peaked, wooden sanctuary ceiling with laminated beams like those in many churches, but the floor is flat and fully carpeted and has no podium or pews. Large, carpeted, movable block risers can be arranged in any configuration and moved anywhere to create a pulpit area. Wooden pew chairs were purchased—sturdy and broad, with upholstered seats and with hymnbook racks underneath. These can be put in any arrangement or stacked on a cart and rolled away. The baptismal pool is sunk into the floor and covered with a heavy, carpeted board so when it is not in use, there is ordinary floor surface above it. The worship arrangement can be set up in any direction. The Sunday school classrooms, kitchen, library, nursery, and church office are along three sides with the main entrance on the fourth. There is no fellowship hall because the sanctuary is a multi-purpose room. The design is both handsome and functional, a creative use of space.

As the building plans took shape, the Lampeter people began to look for a full-time pastor. Earl Kurtz's commitment was only through May of 1980. Since the beginning the Lampeter spirit had been to do things well. Now as they looked for leadership, they decided they wanted one of the most experienced pastors in the denomination.

They settled on Curtis Dubble, pastor of the large First Church of the Brethren in York, Pennsylvania.

Curtis was interested, but he knew the transition from one of the largest churches to a small, new congregation would be difficult. He decided he would propose some conditions. A new church is not yet fully formed; perhaps he could set some patterns of discipleship that are difficult to persuade larger, established congregations to follow. So he told the Lampeter committee that if he were pastor there would be five things he would want: (1) "that a least fifty percent of the core group try on for size the practice of tithing, and that we would help new members through teaching and example to grow to the place where they too within five years would tithe;" (2) "that at least fifty percent of the deacons join me in visiting new people;" (3) "that our evangelism approach include some form of visitation, some form of sharing our faith, and some form of social action;" (4) "that we would lift up as important for Christian growth these additional disciplines: regularity of worship, the study of the the Word, and fellowship;" (5) "that the church would provide a secretary."

"Churches were always telling the district executive and the prospective pastor what they wanted in a minister," Curtis says. "I just felt if I was going to venture out, why shouldn't I as a pastor say, 'This is what I'd like to see in a church.'" The Lampeter people liked Curtis's conditions. He was a bit surprised. "I had to say yes!" he says ruefully. In January of 1980, it was announced that Curtis had been called, and on May 4, he was installed.

One week earlier, on the last Sunday in April, the congregation gave a fond farewell to Earl Kurtz. Because he was so heavily involved in the building program, they asked him to continue to help the committee even though he would no longer be pastor. But always the professional, Earl declined. He knew this was Curtis's job now. It was still possible for Curtis to have some input.

Early in June, the plans were released for bids. On July 27, ground was broken. Throughout the fall and winter, members of the congregation volunteered their Saturdays to work on the building. These work sessions saved money but they also became great times for fellowship. "More important than the building itself," says Bob Frick, "was the process of getting it. That united us."

At Christmas time that year the congregation went caroling through the streets of Lampeter. "It was bitter cold," Bob remembers. "For our last stop we went out to the church. We went through the field, up to the building. There was plastic hanging up because there were no doors. We went in and each person lit a candle. We stood there and sang Christmas carols. I get all choked up just talking about it. That was so moving!" On April 5, 1981, their third anniversary, the congregation moved into their new building, and on May 17, it was dedicated.

In a little over three years Lampeter went from a dream in the minds of the Mechanic Grove Brethren to a fully developed congregation with a beautiful building, a full-time pastor, a membership of 102, and an average attendance of 130. The building cost more than $550,000. The district and General Board came through on their promise of $400,000. Within a year of completion, Lampeter had paid off its portion of the cost and was debt free. The church implemented the five goals that Curtis introduced and has quickly established a fully developed program. Its steady growth has continued and at the beginning of 1984 it has 136 members and an average attendance of 149. In the stewardship area, it has one of the highest per capita giving averages in the denomination. It is made up of a 2 to 1 mix of people from Brethren and non-Brethren backgrounds. According to Earl Ziegler, a total of 61 persons left Mechanic Grove either to join or to support Lampeter within the new church's first two years. Mechanic Grove has replaced all the members it gave up and again needs more space. Instead of building, it is planning to help start another new congregation, this time in the area around Gap.

There were many things that made Lampeter grow—Earl Ziegler's vision and drive and his ability to step back and let Lampeter go; the constant and generous support of Mechanic Grove; pastors who had the right gifts at the right time; backing from the largest and richest district in the Brotherhood; and a heavy concentration of nearby Brethren churches. Unlike most new churches, they did not develop their identity around a pastor/developer but developed a style of strong, independent lay leadership from the first. Their adjustment was not to the leaving of a founding pastor but to the arrival of their first full-time one. In that lay leadership they had an aggressive, demanding administrator, a scatter-brained visionary who was ready to try anything, a little lady with a Pennsylvania Dutch accent who made it her business to make everyone feel welcome, a math teacher who was willing to learn how to be church treasurer, young families eager for a church home, men and women of quiet faith who always believed the church would succeed—it was a good mix, almost everything needed to make a church.

Naomi Wenger, unlike her son Clarence, believed in the project from the first and left Mechanic Grove to be a founding member. She says, "The Lord said to Abraham, 'Go and I will bless you and I will make you a blessing.' Well, that same call comes to us. And I think that too is what this church was built on. We just too often believe that those things were for 'them people.' But they're not! They're for us also! That's the way I see it. So you'll never know what a blessing this has been to the community and is still being, just because they decided to venture out."

With the establishment of Lampeter, the first burst of new church activity ended. Between April, 1978 and mid-1981, there were no new churches started. These four churches have in common a full-time pastor, a new building, strong district support, Brotherhood support, growing membership, and a good future. But they sprouted spontaneously out of different soils: the determination of a dying district to live, the desire of a battered remnant to belong, the settled purpose of a stubborn district to stay on its course, the decision of a local church to venture out. They were not connected to each other. They just grew up by themselves.

CHAPTER TWO
A PIVOTAL TIME

Between the spring of 1978 when Lampeter began and the late summer of 1981, there were, strictly speaking, no new churches started. During this period all four of the churches already underway were establishing their programs and building their structures. By mid-1981, all four had completed this. Two of them, Christ the Servant and Good Shepherd, were already self-supporting. It was almost as though, after a flurry of activity, new church development was catching its breath. Four churches in three years (1976-78)—that was considerable activity for a small denomination not geared up to start churches. Maybe there was a kind of inner wisdom in this interruption, but if so, it occurred without anyone's noting it or intending it. There was as yet no awareness of a movement.

It is not quite correct, however, to imply that there was no church development activity during this period. There were two efforts which, while not quite new churches, were projects that started over after the end of something else.

In August, 1978, in the Mid-Atlantic district, the Broadfording congregation, after a long period of tension, withdrew from the denomination over differences in theology, polity, and ministerial style. There were a number of people from that church who wanted to stay in the Church of the Brethren, and there were also people who had left over the years as the congregation had gone its increasingly independent way. These people wanted to continue a Church of the Brethren in the area. In September, 1978, the district called them together for a meeting. This and subsequent meetings led to a decision to re-form the Broadfording congregation.

On February 4, 1979, this group began to meet in the Community Center in Maugansville, Maryland. The ministers of the district provided pulpit supply until October when John Hostetter was called to be part-time pastor. The church grew and in March, 1980, moved to the Wacohu Grange Hall at Huyetts Crossroads. In December of that year they purchased a six-acre tract at Cearfoss, and in June, 1983, they broke ground for their new church building. John Hostetter was made full-time pastor in the summer of 1982. At the beginning of 1984, they had a membership of 103 and an attendance of 60.

Though the new Broadfording church does not add a congregation to the Church of the Brethren and really comes from a remnant of one that was lost, its people have had to start almost from scratch and go through most of the steps a new church goes through. This they have done without the bitterness that might be expected from a bruised remnant. Their vision does not feed on regret for what they were or anger at what they lost, but on appreciation of what they are and enthusiasm for what they are becoming. The Mid-Atlantic district has nurtured this project as they would a new church.

The other project has an equally unusual history. In 1964, somewhat to their embarrassment, the Church of the Brethren had to close the mother church in the United States, the Germantown congregation in Philadelphia. A presence was continued through an effective community ministry, but no congregation gathered in the Germantown church for 16 years. Then in March, 1980, the Germantown Ministry Board decided to hire a full-time pastor and begin a congregation again.

What had existed before and had come to an end was a middle-class, white congregation that had dwindled as the neighborhood turned black. What was envisioned now was an inner-city church that would serve the whole community, which is mixed, but especially the blacks, who are the predominant group. In April, Fredric M. Jenkins was called to be the pastor. He began his work in the summer of 1980.

Since then this small church has struggled. The transition from a community ministry to a congregation was not smooth, and some mistakes were made. The church has not grown, and its membership and attendance are very small. This congregation is important, not only because it is being replanted where Brethren first started their life in the new world but because Brethren need to learn how to start and nurture inner-city churches where neighborhoods are changing or deteriorating, as well as suburban churches where subdivisions are growing.

Aside from these two projects, there were no new churches started for almost three and a half years. But during this time two things happened that drew the attention of Brethren to new church development.

Late in 1978, the Goals and Budget Committee of the General Board began to set objectives for the 1980s. This was part of a Brotherhood-wide effort to set "Goals for the 80s." The objectives were to be specific and measurable instances of the more general and inspirational "Goals." While these objectives were being discussed, the Parish Ministries Commission hired Merle Crouse in January, 1979 to be the full-time church development consultant. This decision represented a major change in priorities.

When Hubert Newcomer held the church development responsibilities, they were a small part of his job. They entailed primarily the ministry support which districts could request (hence the contacts made by Florida/Puerto Rico for Christ the Servant and by Northern Ohio for Trinity) and facility development funds. Neither of these was restricted to new church development, though both kinds of support could be used for that purpose and were. Hubert resigned his position in 1977 and for a year these responsibilities were carried by Lyle Lichtenberger. Lyle's death in the fall of 1978 left the position open again.

It was at this time that the objective-setting process began. There was a feeling among General Board members that it was time to start new churches again. On the General Board staff, Bob Neff, the General Secretary, and Ralph McFadden, Executive Secretary of the Parish Ministries Commission, were convinced that this was the right direction for the denomination. When it came time to fill Lyle Lichtenberger's position, the decision was made to make a full-time position in new church development and hire Merle Crouse.

Merle was already a part-time General Board employee. His responsibilities as the Florida/Puerto Rico district executive had always been one-third time, and with the other two-thirds of his time he had been serving as Latin America representative. He resigned his Florida/Puerto Rico position, and all his energies were shifted to new church development. Now he was in a position to continue on a larger scale the work he had started in Florida. The ministry support and facility development funds were put under his responsibility and were directed primarily, but not exclusively, to new church development.

So Merle had a directive and he had funds. Then in the fall of 1979, the General Board gave him an objective as well—15 new church starts by the end of 1984. Quickly Merle got to work. He visited Lampeter twice as they entered their building program, and eventually the General Board, on his recommendation, committed $25,000 to the Lampeter building, as well as $8,000 in ministerial support. He began to work with Trinity, which was already receiving ministerial support. The General Board gave $25,000 toward Trinity's building, and it was Merle who urged Trinity to complete the work and who came up with 5,000 additional General Board dollars to help them do it.

Merle made himself available as a consultant to any district, group, or congregation considering a new church. As new church planting got underway again in 1981, there was no project that Merle was not in contact with, and each new congregation was counted toward that goal of 15. It could be said that by the beginning of the 1980s the Church of the Brethren had, if not a movement, at least a denominational program in new church development.

But the projects that were started as new church planting got underway again in 1981 did not arise out of these decisions at the top. They continued to grow spontaneously out of districts and local churches and the determination of individuals who were convinced that it was time for Brethren to get moving.

One of these people was Jim Myer, farmer, free minister, and elder in the White Oak congregation in Lancaster County, Pennsylvania and a leader in the Brethren Revival Fellowship (BRF), an informal organization of individuals and churches concerned with preserving and defending traditional Brethren values. This group has held to the pattern of the free ministry (ministers are called out of the congregation and support themselves through secular vocations), plain dress, church discipline, and a literal interpretation of the scripture. In a period when the Church of the Brethren has been changing, the BRF has been calling Brethren back to the old ways.

"I am still primarily unhappy with the way people of the liberal theology and persuasion go about conducting the church," Jim Myer said in a sermon he preached in 1980, "but I have not seen among the conservative Churches of the Brethren much of an example of success in evangelism or mission work either. We seem to be on somewhat of a retreat. Why isn't it high time, with all the resources that we have in some of our congregations, to be out actually on the field in an offensive effort." Jim Myer's challenge inspired a new congregation—unique among the new churches because it is a BRF church and unusual in another way—because it is in New England, where before 1981 the Brethren never had a church.

The story of this church began in 1975 when the leaders of Brethren Volunteer Service (BVS) came to the BRF people and asked why they no longer sent their young people to BVS. The answer was that BRF youth in BVS were "losing their faith," coming back with unacceptable ideas. BVS offered to create special units where BRF people could do the training, choose the projects, and provide house parents. "It was an offer we couldn't turn down," Jim Myer says. The first BRF unit was placed in 1976 at the Voice of Calvary Ministry in Jackson, Mississippi. In 1977 Jim Myer and Mervin Keller, who was in charge of BVS recruiting for BRF and also a farmer/minister at White Oak, flew to Maine to investigate the possibility of a second site. That visit and two subsequent visits resulted in the placement in February, 1979 of a BRF BVS unit at the Lewiston Housing Authority in Lewiston, Maine. Three volunteers plus the house parents and their small son moved into a large apartment in the middle of the Hillview public housing project. They were to do maintenance and secretarial work.

Lewiston is an unlikely place for conservative Brethren whose families have long histories in the Pennsylvania German sectarian subculture. Lewiston is a predominantly Catholic, old industrial city made up mostly of people of French Canadian descent. Everybody—the Lewiston Housing Authority people and the BRF leaders—wondered what this mix would bring.

The volunteers were strictly enjoined against proselytizing. Their ministry was to be a service ministry. The staff of the housing authority were leery of these religious people. There had been trouble in the projects with aggressive Jehovah's Witnesses. Were these people going to be like that? Were they some kind of a cult? The first volunteers quietly went about their work. They were hard workers, honest to a fault, and very conscientious. These qualities impressed the housing authority people. Still they did not know what to make of the volunteers' quiet, forebearing ways, their strict prohibitions against smoking, drinking, and the movies, and the prayer covering worn by the women and girls. They were curious about these Brethren, yet afraid to ask questions for fear of a sermon.

"It fascinated me that they were not forward," Marilyn Bourget, housing authority staff member, says, "that they would talk of their faith only if the door opened. Their actions, their way of living, were really a demonstration of their faith."

The Lewiston Housing Authority staff were so pleased with this first unit that they gladly accepted the second unit in February of 1980. As this unit was settling in, the director of LHA said to Jim Myer, "I don't want to tell you how to run your program, but some of our people here at Lewiston, the residents [of the projects], were just beginning to open up to your house parents last year about their problems, and then their year of service was up and they had to go home. It might be more effective for you if your houseparents could stay longer than just one year at a time." "It seems to me," Jim Myer said in his 1980 sermon, "that God has turned some hearts and minds of some people around even in one year. It almost sounds like an invitation to come—'We want to hear more.'"

Jim knew the man was not thinking of a church, and he knew that a church could not be started in the housing authority, but he interpreted this as encouragement to establish a more permanent presence in Lewiston. A church seemed a good way to do this. Actually, Jim had had the idea of a church in mind as early as the first overtures in Maine. "I always believed service should not be divorced from evangelism," Jim says. "The two should go hand in hand. The evangelist and the good Samaritan can and should be one and the same person. We have lost many opportunities for establishing churches where BVSers were. When people realize you are there genuinely to give of yourself, not to get something in return, they are more inclined to open up to you."

Jim took his idea to the BRF Committee. They favored the plan, though none of them had been involved in starting a new church. They knew it would take a big effort. Jim, in his own words, "mustered enough courage to make a motion that we plan to start a church by the spring of 1981." The motion was passed unanimously, and the committee gave Jim the job of promotion chairman for the project.

Jim took a map, drew a line from east to west in the eastern half of Pennsylvania, and picked seven churches along that line. They were all served by the free ministry, all were tradition-minded. They were compatible with each other and sympathetic to BRF goals and values. BRF is an informal organization representing the viewpoints of all who want to support it. Great authority is vested in the BRF Committee to speak for the group. There is no membership list of either individuals or congregations. Once authorized by the committee, Jim Myer was free to pick as few or as many churches as seemed right. He sought what he thought would be the proper amount and mix of support to make the project go. In the spring of 1980 he preached at each of the seven churches. His sermon was entitled "Mission in the State of Maine," and in it he issued his challenge.

Preaching from the story of Abraham in Genesis 12, he said, "There is a tendency in congregations back home to become ingrown and settled and complacent and at ease. And oftentimes when that's happening, the devil has some subtle inroads to begin to plant poison and unbelief in the local church because it's sort of resting on past efforts. It's not really alert." His own congregation, White Oak, the largest and strongest of the BRF churches, was one of the seven, and when he preached the sermon there, he said, "Sometimes I get the impression that we as a congregation don't need to move out. We don't really need to have this kind of disturbing project, because we don't even need the denomination very much. We're big enough. We can sort of go it on our own. But the biblical pattern is to go out!"

Jim went only once to each church. He gave what he calls "a rather long, forceful sermon." He did not give an opportunity to ask questions. He did leave with the elder a sheet of paper with five things he wanted from each church if they became sponsors of the project: that they would look on it with favor; that they would pray for it; that they would be open to encouraging members to go as workers; that they would agree to share resources—talent, involvement, money; that they would select a person to serve on a Maine Mission Committee. He left his telephone number and asked anyone interested in the project to call him.

What Jim and the BRF had in mind was the colonization method of starting a new church. Jim was asking in his sermon for people who were willing to move to Lewiston permanently and to become the nucleus of a church. He was really issuing two calls—first to the churches, asking for their official support; second to individuals, asking them to pull up roots like Abraham and go to a strange country. He felt the project needed the support of at least five of the seven churches. This was to be a sign to him. If fewer responded, it meant the project was not rightly conceived. Six of the churches voted to back it. The Maine Mission Committee was formed and began to make plans.

The first people to respond to the call were John and June Stauffer. They owned a lawn and garden machinery business in eastern Lancaster County and were members of the Spring Grove congregation at Blue Ball. They were in the process of liquidating their business, selling their property, and buying another house when they heard Jim Myer speak at the Spring Grove church. John had a dream of being a missionary, and this was especially on his mind at the time. He wanted to know what kind of project Jim Myer had in mind. "I couldn't find fault with the project he presented," John says. "My calling and his presentation just locked right into each other."

The decision was not so smooth and quick for June, who thought about leaving family and friends and being uprooted. Because they were between properties anyway, they made a trip to Lewiston within a month of hearing the sermon. Unexpectedly, they found a house and bought it, and John found a job. Six weeks later, in August, 1980, they moved. It happened very quickly, and they were on site in the Lewiston area almost a year before the other families arrived. The Stauffers felt that the quick opening of the way was a sure sign that this was the right direction for their life. "When I'm not following God's will, then I have to look for ways to be self-sufficient, to take care of myself, to plan ahead," John says. "But if I put it in God's hands, it's like going up a ladder. I just have to step on the rung and make the next move."

The decision also came quickly for Marlin and Carol Fahnestock. Marlin was a carpenter and Carol took care of their home and children, held a job as a part-time nurse's aide, and also ran a small consignment business out of their home. They had just built a new house. They too had felt the call to be in mission work. Over the years they had considered many projects. But none had seemed right. This one was different. "It just hit us like a ton of stones," says Carol. "I told my husband this has got to be our project. We were a unity. We both felt this was where the Lord wanted us to go."

Through the rest of 1980, only the Stauffers and Fahnestocks were definitely committed to the project. And one of the most important components of the project was still not in place. There was no minister. Merv Keller had begun to feel an inner prompting, a sense that this might be his calling. He and Jim Myer had even talked about the matter, but in a very offhand manner. In the tradition of the free ministry, a person regardless of how strongly he feels called never puts himself forward. The call must come from the church. So Merv did nothing about his feelings except pray about them. In October, he did attend a special meeting for interested persons, but only at the invitation of Jim Myer.

After that meeting Merv began to pray seriously about the call. He and his wife Karen did not really want to go to Maine, especially Karen. They had just completely remodeled their house. Merv owned his farm, enjoyed farming, and was successful at it. But he still felt inner nudges. "I did not want my farm to tie me down to this earth," he says. "My prayer was that the Maine Mission Committee vote unanimously in favor of me if I'm to be the one. That was my signal from God. I didn't want this to be something Jim Myer concocted. He thought I should be the one. That was very much on my mind that night when we came home."

By this time Jim and Merv were not talking about it at all. It is not proper even for a minister and elder to exercise overt personal influence on another's call. In December, Jim Myer and his wife invited Merv and Karen to have dinner with them at the Leola Family Restaurant. After the meal Jim formally invited Merv on behalf of the Maine Mission Committee to be the spiritual leader of the mission. He announced that this was the decision not only of the eight people on the committee but of the members of the BRF Committee and the White Oak Committee on Mission as well. "He said there were 20 men who unanimously approved it," Merv reports. He remembers feeling, "Wow, Lord! You're really trying to make this clear!"

In March of 1981, Dennis and Mary Jane Myer from the Spring Grove congregation went to Lewiston to be the house parents for the third BVS unit. They too had heard Jim Myer's sermon. The project did not jump out at him, Dennis says, but the idea grew in his thoughts. It was a good time to move because a business commitment had just ended. Being house parents would give them an opportunity to test out the idea before deciding. The decision was harder for Mary Jane, who had close family ties. By early summer, they had made up their minds, and they bought a house and prepared to move into it when the BVS unit ended.

There was another White Oak family struggling with the call—Jim and Lois Minnich. Jim owned a successful masonry business. In fact, at that time he was the masonry contractor of the new White Oak church building. Lois remembers that Jim was feeling a void in his life. He had worked on a volunteer construction unit. He had driven a truck with relief clothing. They had talked of some day serving as house parents in Maine.

Jim Myer's sermon had no particular effect on the Minnichs. But he began to talk to Jim Minnich about the project. When Jim Myer went to Maine on a ministerial visit, he invited the Minnichs to go along. Lois fought the idea at first, but it was she who first made up her mind. Jim was still undecided.

On January 4, 1981, in an emotional moment during the Sunday morning service, it was announced at White Oak that Merv Keller would be the Maine Mission minister. "Jim looked at me and I at him," Lois remembers. "I knew right then Jim had made up his mind. He had wanted to know who the spiritual leader was. That following week he called the realtor and put the house on the market."

The project now had a minister and his family, three other families, a fifth family that was probable, and a sixth, Shannon and Marian Negley from the Upton congregation, who were planning to be the 1982 house parents and were possible candidates.

Up to this point, the initiative on this project had been entirely with the BRF. The six churches were located in two districts, Atlantic Northeast and Southern Pennsylvania. Jim Myer had kept the district executives informed of the plans and progress, but there had been no request for financial support or official sponsorship. Likewise, there had been contact with Merle Crouse representing the Brotherhood. Merle had accompanied Jim on one of his trips to Lewiston, and together they had done a feasibility study. The results were not very positive. Lewiston was not a growing community. Culturally, it was not a place where people receptive to the BRF message would be found. But because the project was being started without a large outlay of funds, Merle thought it would have a fair chance. He supported the initiative and effort of the BRF.

On May 31, 1981, all this effort and soul-searching came together in an emotional commissioning service for the six families. It was held at White Oak, and the two district executives were invited to give the commissioning prayer, during which they were assisted by the elder in the laying-on-of-hands. Afterwards, the members of the audience gave the Chautauqua Salute, the waving of white handkerchiefs that used to be the traditional Annual Conference sendoff for Brethren missionaries.

In June, the Minnichs moved. On the same day in July, the Kellers and Fahnestocks moved. These moves were made with caravans of cars and trucks, as family and friends in the church turned out to help and to accompany them north. On August 2, 1981, this small Brethren colony in French Canadian Lewiston held its first Sunday morning worship service in the Hillview community building. Merv spoke from the same text Jim Myer had used in his "Mission in the State of Maine" address—Genesis 12. Two Sundays later, the little fellowship moved to the basement of the Captain's Hall, a fish market in Lewiston, where they met until May of 1982, when they approached the Jewish congregation about renting their empty synagogue, recently vacated for a new building. Their lease/purchase offer for one year with an option to buy for $75,000 was accepted. On June 20, they held their first service there. Except for the Hebrew tablets carved over the main entrance, the plain, simple red brick building looks much like a Church of the Brethren built perhaps 50 years ago.

The question almost everyone has—both BRF supporters and Brethren who do not agree with the BRF—is, how are these conservative Brethren fitting in? How are they being received? Can they grow in Lewiston? Calvin Rich, a bushy-haired, bearded Maine native who lived neighbors to the Kellers, says, "These people are just some of the nicest people I've ever met in my life. They are honest, hardworking, good people. They are in touch with what life is all about." Sandra Dollar, who lives across the road from the Fahnestocks and who has become one of Carol's closest friends, is impressed with the closeness of the families and with the fact that the Brethren volunteer to do things in the community. She was impressed to see the people who came all the way from Pennsylvania just to help Marlin and Carol move. Paul Veillieux, former administrator of the housing authority, thinks they have done an excellent job of getting into the community.

And the "colonizers" themselves seem to enjoy being in a new environment. Most of them had never lived away from the home area. Merv Keller likes the challenge of pastoring a church; and during this initial period, the BRF is helping to support him with a two-thirds salary, so that unlike other free ministers he does not need to make a full living but can devote himself to raising up the church. They have invited friends and neighbors to worship with them. They have had special singing services. People who visit them feel welcome. They seem to feel comfortable in Maine and the people there accept them and like them.

But there is a second question more difficult to answer. Will people join the church? Can it grow? Calvin Rich, whose admiration for them is so great, asks frankly, "Are these people just so remote theologically speaking that they are out of step?" Paul Veillieux is more optimistic, "I believe it [the church] will grow. I believe there are certainly new people who decide to switch from one group to another. They [The Brethren] have done a masterful job in the year and a half they've been working." But to the question, how will people receive the BRF disciplines, he answers. "I hear a lot of extreme conservatism. To find people who are willing to go into that particular kind of attitude, I think, is going to be tough. Certainly if you're going to start asking some of the women to wear the headpiece—that is going to be extremely hard. The wearing of blue jeans, the wearing of wild clothes, the going to dances, the watching of television—I think families around here have been doing this for a long, long time. It's hard to break habits. So I think it's going to be tough in this community, but there are people out there who are willing to sacrifice."

Perhaps of all the people the Maine project has touched, Marilyn Bourget has been the most deeply affected. She became close friends with Melody Stahl, a BVSer in the 1980 unit. She was an active Catholic and Lewiston native. After she got over her initial resistance, she was fascinated by the Brethren and their faith. Over lunch and sometimes even over dictation, Melody and Marilyn would have long discussions. They would search the Bible together. Marilyn would ask questions sometimes that Melody could not answer and she would go back to the BVS apartment at night and the volunteers would pray together and then pour over the scriptures to find answers for Marilyn. One night at an evangelistic meeting in the nearby town of Greene, Marilyn experienced a deep change and went forward at the altar call. Melody and another volunteer named Mary were there. "We cried all the way home," Marilyn remembers. "It was beautiful. We woke everybody up at the BVS apartment. We stood in the kitchen and had prayer together. My faith has grown a lot because of the BVS people. They're very special."

When Marilyn heard that the Brethren were starting a church, she remembers thinking, "They have to be crazy! To uproot whole families! They'll meet resistance from the local people." Then she adds, "I struggled long and hard, not joining a church until they arrived because I thought maybe I would like to join the Church of the Brethren. But there were just a lot of traditions in their church that I felt were restrictive for me, and having been freed from all the man-made rules, I just had some real problems with joining that church."

Dennis Myer, who is one of the deacons in the new fellowship, comments on the importance of being true to their convictions. "I do not feel the covering [prayer veil for women] is a matter of salvation. I see it as something that is consistent with our beliefs. We are biblicists, trying to follow the truths in the Bible. If we let one point go, what's to say we can't let another point go. It's an endless road once you get started." Jim Myer says, "We know that the type of church standards we aim to maintain will limit fast growth. That's not a high priority. We're more interested in quality than quantity." But he also talks about hopes for two more fellowships by 1991. "We want a faithful church, but we also want an outgoing church. It's easy to go in either direction. You can say, 'We want growth at any cost.' Or you can say, 'We want faithfulness, and if we don't grow, it doesn't matter.' But my view is that we want the faithfulness and the growth, although we know that the two work against each other somewhat."

The Lewiston Brethren have added nine new members since moving to Maine; three are children from the "colonizing" families; six are Lewiston area residents, three of whom have Church of the Brethren background. These people are deeply appreciative of the faith community they have found. The fellowship is supported generously by the six churches in Pennsylvania. Jim Myers is the elder-in-charge and makes regular visits for oversight. The Lewiston Brethren eventually purchased the synagogue building, and the Negleys have moved up permanently. On October 9, the Atlantic Northeast district conference took official action to recognize the group as a fellowship. The congregation is on its way. Dennis Myer says, "Our responsibility is to be faithful, to sow the seed, to invite people, to share with them spiritual truths, but God is the one who has to call the people. His Spirit opens up truths, convicts of sin, calls to salvation. I still have the faith to believe that God has us here for a purpose. Maybe that purpose is only five or ten years down the road. We are getting our roots in now. But in the meantime we still have the responsibility to share our faith."

Almost all the new churches have been well-planned, but the congregation in Blacksburg, Virginia stands out as a textbook case. As early as 1973 there was talk in southern Virginia of starting new churches, and some bold plans were discussed. But nothing was done.

Then in 1978, the witness commission of the district board took up the issue again. Owen Stultz, the district executive, had been urging new church work at the earlier date. Now it was he again who nudged the witness commission. In October, they made a recommendation which the district board voted to carry to district conference: "That we move as rapidly as possible toward the establishment of a new congregation in Virlina district, with a progress report to be given to the 1979 district conference, including definite plans as to location, time schedule, methods of development, and plan of financing." The district conference passed the recommendation and the witness commission appointed a new church extension committee to carry out the ambitious agenda.

Merle Crouse was quickly contacted, and by April of 1979 the committee had already met with him twice. One of those meetings included Don Robinson, who was asked to do a feasibility study. The committee decided to adopt the philosophy of church extension that Don Robinson proposed, which was to look for a growing area and to invest "substantially" in "the strongest of leadership" and "very adequate facilities." The estimated cost to the district was to be $250,000.

Don studied six areas and recommended Montgomery County, in the southwestern part of Virginia, where the state dips down under West Virginia. There in the small city of Blacksburg (pop. 30,638), where Virginia Tech with its 21,500 students is found, Don called the church extension committee's attention particularly to the Hethwood development on the outskirts of the city. At the entrance to Hethwood, the developers, the Snyder-Hunt Corporation, had set aside 3.7 acres of land zoned for a church. The site was ideal. It was overpriced in the opinion of the committee, but they had an experienced real estate agent and appraiser among their membership and were confident they could negotiate. The asking price was $30,000 per acre or approximately $110,000. They offered $50,000, and the developers came down to $75,000. A bargain was struck, subject to district conference approval.

By including the site purchase plan, the church extension committee took to the 1979 district conference a more detailed and definite progress report than they had expected. Their report was accepted, and they were authorized to purchase the lot. They signed the contract to purchase in early January. In the meantime, they had begun to organize a fund-raising campaign, and they called on David Holl, pastor of the Ninth Street Church of the Brethren in Roanoke, former professional fund-raiser and college development director, to head the operation. They set a goal of $225,000 and kicked off the campaign in January. Each church in the district was contacted (some 80 congregations) and asked for a pledge. The response was more enthusiastic than anyone expected, and $236,000 was committed. The pledges were to be paid over a 30-month period to begin July 1.

The Virlina Brethren seem to be good at delegating authority, and that helped make the process move smoothly. The project originated in the witness commission. Since this group has many responsibilities, a church extension committee was created to handle the research, planning, and funding. But church extension is broader than any one project, so early in 1980 when the campaign was in full swing, a Blacksburg steering committee was created specifically to supervise the new project. This was done early enough in the process so that the steering committee could also function as the pastoral search committee and then work closely with the pastor as soon as he arrived on site.

A second important move was to name Don Flory chairperson of the steering committee. Don brought a church development background to the position. In the late 1950s he had been pastor of the Brook Park church, one of those four new congregations started by the Northern Ohio district. He was excited about starting new churches again and was full of ideas about how to avoid some of the mistakes of that earlier period. There was a second reason he was a good choice. Sometimes the closest Church of the Brethren is threatened by a new congregation and fears losing members. One of the nearby churches in Lancaster County, Pennsylvania, had this fear when Lampeter was started. The Brethren congregation closest to Blacksburg was the Christiansburg church, where Don Flory was the pastor. Making Don head of the steering committee assured his support and the backing of the Christiansburg church.

Norman estimates that he knocked on five to six hundred doors in that initial period. Sometimes he went back two or three times until he found someone home. He was invited into approximately two out of ten households where someone was at home. In about six of ten cases the people at least opened the door and talked briefly. In only one case was he treated rudely. The Lutheran method counsels a very short visit, and Norman followed that advice, except for a few especially interesting visits that stretched much longer.

Norman tells many anecdotes about his door-knocking, the people he met, and the later relationships that resulted. He says about half of the people in the fellowship in the first year came through these visits. "Norman knocked on our door about three days after we moved in," Torsten Sponenberg says. "Phil, my husband, was taking a nap so we asked him to come back. We had not heard of the Church of the Brethren. When he came the second time, I was out of town." Phil takes up the story, "We had a conversation and seemed to have a lot of theological points in common. I grilled him and he grilled me. We came from a small church, and we were hoping to find a large church where we could sit on the back pew and be ignored. After he knocked on the door, I really prayed about it. I think God has a sense of humor. To be in town two days and then have this guy from this new church knock on your door! It seemed pretty funny. But I think it's where God wanted us to be. He was making sure we didn't make any other commitments."

The next step was to organize two small study groups for the people who expressed interest in the church. Norman called these GO Groups (Growth and Outreach Groups), where Bible studies were held and the Church of the Brethren was introduced. Norman used audiovisuals and printed materials to enrich his explanations. These GO Groups met through the summer of 1981. One of their purposes was to prepare the interested people for the first worship. Because there would be members of their own GO Group there, they would not feel like strangers. The two groups coming together would become the nucleus of the worshiping community. From these groups Norman selected three people to help him plan the first worship. They became the service committee. They would advise Norman and gradually take over responsibility from the district steering committee. Eventually they could become the nucleus for the church board.

Following this procedure, never rushing it, placing one block on top of another, Norman was ready by early October to begin worship. According to the method, the service committee was to look for a place to meet, but the district had already done some advance work and had arranged with the developers to use the Huntsman Community Center in Hethwood. This has a large, comfortable, carpeted room with a cathedral ceiling, a small kitchenette, and sliding glass doors that open to a swimming pool—an excellent temporary setting. On September 13, 1981, after three years of smooth development, Good Shepherd church opened its doors. Thirty-six people attended.

In his 1979 feasibility study, Don Robinson wrote, "If a church is to go in that area, it will have to be a different type of church than we Brethren are used to. It will need to be cosmopolitan and strictly suburban, with the ability to appeal to a wide range of people. Because of the university the educational level in that area is very high. Thus the church would need a great deal of sophistication in carrying out its ministry." Norman's early experience bears out Don's analysis. Of the first four families to get involved, all were connected with the university. The Blacksburg fellowship's tasks is twofold: to be urbane enough to interest people from the university while being grounded in the New Testament and in Brethren traditions and to be a church home for the Brethren students at Virginia Tech, who number about ninety at any given time. The group has more variety in it than some. It also has a greater turnover.

Jim Craig, professor of geological sciences at the university and a member of the service committee, says of the church, "This is not like an average community. Now, I know there is a new church in Carol Stream, Illinois. I don't think it's a college community, which means it's very different in two aspects. One, there is not a large influx of students who are temporary, kind of ebbing and flowing with the school year. We require a balance in a church like this, where we serve the students and the families as well. It's not just a family church. The other aspect is that most of the people in a community like this are not from here. Very few of us have roots in any immediate vicinity. The college community brings in all these families from other places. You don't have a root structure, which means again then that the people are more heterogeneous than they would be say in the Shenandoah Valley or probably in an area like Carol Stream, Illinois. We've also had a great opportunity in this multi-faceted community to sample other nationalities as well as other religions. There were the Korean family and the visitors from Nigeria and Thailand. There are just many, many people we wouldn't have if this were a more average community."

Speaking about how he came into the fellowship, Jim Craig says, "I called Norman. We lived in an area where he did not come around knocking on doors. We had come out of a Methodist background but had for several years attended a non-denominational church. But we always had felt that was a temporary situation. My wife teaches a Bible study in Christiansburg and had known many Church of the Brethren women. She was impressed by their service aspect, by their true love for each other, and by their concern for other people and their problems. We felt God was leading us back into a mainline church. So I called the Harshes. They came over and we chatted. I asked if I could look at some books. I knew nothing about the Church of the Brethren. Norman gave me a rather large stack of things. There were many questions in my mind. We very much found ourselves in agreement with the ideas of the church, the theology, and the warmth of the people involved. We could agree with what they were trying to do and with the fact that they were trying to expand Christ into the community in the service of people's lives. Two specific things come to mind that the Brethren bring to this area. One would be the aspect of service. The other would be that the Brethren church is a traditional peace church. There are few peace churches in this vicinity."

Commenting on the future of the church, Jim Craig says, "I think everyone in the church has really prayed constantly that we would move at the will of the Lord, not at our will. We become impatient. We want to do it in our way. We want to see 300 people in this room on a Sunday. It's not the numbers of people that count. Not to say that numbers aren't important, but it's the quality of the service, and it's that the people come out of a true sense of commitment and that we can handle each one, that we can share the gospel with them. There are groups that count numbers only. There are many 'numbers' who probably are never saved. We want people to come to the Lord and to accept Christ as their Savior. That's what's really important."

The Good Shepherd people combine a desire for personal salvation with a commitment to service and peace. They are open to the cultural and religious variety of the university community yet are unapologetically Christian. They support and affirm other churches in the community yet have a strong Brethren identity. They have a personal piety that affirms God's presence in the day-to-day workings of their lives and their congregation. This is a delicate balance of elements that tend to exist separately in congregations with a one-dimensional identity.

In November 1982, Good Shepherd, Blacksburg, was admitted to fellowship status at district conference. Phil Sponenberg, who was a Good Shepherd delegate at the conference, joked with people about his name and their puzzlement because it wasn't a "Brethren" name. Of the early core group only one family had Church of the Brethren background. As the church has grown, it has attracted Brethren students as well as new people from the university and from Norman's contacts. The church experienced a slowing of growth in its second year, not unlike that of Christ the Servant, but it is picking up again. At the beginning of 1984 it has 18 members, 11 associate student members, and an attendance between 35 and 40.

From Owen Stultz to Don Flory to Norman Harsh to the members of the fellowship, the people responsible for Good Shepherd have had a strong sense of providence. Nancy Bowman, an officer in the University's Recruitment and Employment Department and church organist, says, "I think it was God's will that a church be in Blacksburg, Virginia."

By mid-1980, Virlina had all its ducks in a row; it had its location, its land, its funds, its steering committee, and its concept. All it needed was a pastor. The district office announced the position. The steering committee began interviewing. They invited several candidates to come to Blacksburg and view the community and the site. Don Flory talked to Don Shank, pastor at Christ the Servant, who said, as Flory remembers, " 'If he doesn't come to you, you probably don't have the right guy, even if he has the talents you want.' I crossed a number of people off the list on that basis. One candidate, who had good credentials and was an accomplished pastor, asked, 'How do you know it's going to work?' I checked him off the list. I figured if he had to ask that question, he was not going to make it at Blacksburg!"

Norman Harsh, who was then pastor of the East Fairview Church of the Brethren at Manheim, Pennsylvania, heard of the project at Annual Conference in 1980 and expressed interest. Don Flory remembers Norman's interview, "It became evident that Norman's organizational ability, his strong theology, his strong convictions, his strong belief that this was the kind of thing he wanted to do at this point in his ministry were what we wanted. We asked him the same question [the other candidate had asked them], and he said, 'The Blacksburg church exists right at this point in the mind of God alone. This committee is beginning to hope and dream on it, but God alone has a dream of what he wants. That's all there is at this point.' He knew that, but was willing to move into that kind of situation." The steering committee decided on Norman and the district called him. The appointment was announced at the November district conference.

By this time a practice of sending pastor/developers to new church development workshops was being established. All pastors except Curtis Dubble, who took over an already established congregation, had attended one or soon would. But none of them had had the opportunity to do it before assuming his position. The Blacksburg steering committee built this into the schedule. Norman was due to start February 1, 1981. The district moved the Harshs to Blacksburg late in January and then sent them to Milwaukee, Wisconsin, for a weeklong seminar for pastors and spouses, run by the Lutherans. This was a felicitous match. The Brethren, who are a small denomination, cannot operate their own workshops and have to rely on other denominations, sometimes Presbyterians, Methodists, and United Church of Christ, sometimes Lutherans. Though basic principles are the same, each denomination has its own style, and the Lutheran style tends to be very methodical. This fit Norman. He absorbed the Lutheran method, came back to Blacksburg, and carefully put it to work step-by-step. "I am eternally grateful for that workshop. I wouldn't have known the first thing to do," Norman says. "It is a very carefully crafted step-by-step process. You do one thing. When you have that done, you do the next step. You take however long it takes."

The first step is to move in, get acquainted, choose a name, and design a brochure. When the steering committee arrived at Norman's house for their first meeting in the first week of February, Norman had copy ready for the brochure. That night they selected the name Good Shepherd, and the next day Norman took the brochure to the printer. While it was being printed, Norman made appointments with the clergymen in town, the mayor, the police chief, the fire department, and the school board people. He explained who the Brethren are and why they were there. He asked questions and tried to see the community through the eyes of the person he was calling on. He got his picture in the paper and had himself interviewed for the church page. He put up a sign on the church property.

When the brochures were ready, he started knocking on doors. He made it clear to the other pastors that he was not going to steal their members. He asked the nearby Lutheran pastor for the names of the six families from that church who lived in Hethwood. When he called on these people, he reinforced and encouraged their Lutheran ties. Further, when he met someone new who was Lutheran, he gave that family's name to the Lutheran pastor. Quickly, Norman won the trust of the Blacksburg clergy. In fact, as the months passed his ability to talk to both the evangelical and mainline ministers, thus getting them to talk to one another, improved the spirit of the clergy association.

The purpose of Norman's visits was not only to invite people to the new church but to get acquainted with the neighborhood. "Three other pastors live in Hethwood," Norman observes. "Not one of them enjoys the personal relationship with other people in the community that I do." Following the Lutheran method, the pastor does not even think about holding worship until he has covered 80 percent of the mission territory. "Once you start having worship," Norman explains, "your time is used in planning worship services, preparing sermons, and all these kinds of things. You don't have time."

It is ironic that the Brethren, after being in North America more than 250 years and never going to New England, started two new congregations there within a year's time and that these churches are different and similar in such ways that the history of the Brethren in this century can be read in their comparison.

It was in the latter part of August, 1981, only a few days after the Lewiston Brethren held their first worship service, that the Coffmans, Shreckhises, and Grouts arrived in southern Vermont to start a church in the Brattleboro/Putney area. Paul Grout, Dick Shreckhise, and Dennis Coffman are ordained ministers sent as a team by the Southern District of Pennsylvania. Brattleboro is a small city in the green hills where the Brethren are unknown.

Two of these three pastors did not have what might be called a "traditional Brethren" upbringing. Paul and Dorothy Grout had grown up in the Presbyterian church and as young schoolteachers had joined the Church of the Brethren because of its peace stand during the Vietnam War era. Dennis Coffman had grown up in a Church of the Brethren community in Bachmansville, Pennsylvania, but only became active in the church as a teenager. Both made a choice for the Brethren and then, as they grew in the faith, felt a call to the ministry. What makes this important is that they have a keen sense of what the Church of the Brethren has to offer. Over the years some of the best Brethren leadership has · come from people who chose to be "Brethren." They have been among the best at interpreting who the Brethren are and where they should be going.

The roots of the Vermont project go back to the mid-seventies when the three men were students at Bethany Theological Seminary. Because of their concern for spiritual life on campus they began to meet together in the mornings for prayer. They were outspoken, were involved in the social protest issues of the day, and were members of one of the most "rebellious" classes in Bethany's history. They shared a belief that along with the social programs of the church, renewal was needed. Sometimes they dreamed of one day starting a church together or sharing a cooperative ministry of some sort. The idea took different forms, sometimes including one or two other students. But it never became a serious possibility, though it came close enough to make their wives uneasy. After seminary all three took pastorates.

Early in 1978, about three years after graduation, Paul and Dick went back to Bethany for an advanced pastoral seminar, leaving their families together at the Grouts' home in Michigan, where Paul was pastor of the Sugar Ridge Church of the Brethren. After the seminar Dick and Paul joined their families for a few more days of visiting. "One evening," Dick remembers, "Paul and I went out for a walk. Paul said to me, 'Well, Dick, what's next? Do we go on from here and take another church? Same kind of situation or what? I'm not ready to leave here, but just what's next for us?' I said, 'I don't know, Paul. Maybe we ought to go somewhere together and start a new church.' He said, 'That's just what I was going to say!' We got to talking about it and Paul said, 'Say something to Dennis. Tell him we talked seriously. See if he's interested. Let's at least start praying about it and be open for it.' I went and shared that with Dennis. 'Are you ready to move?' Dennis said. It was like he was ready to pack up and do it right now. I think from that point on we pretty much knew it was going to happen sometime."

That was in the spring of 1978. That fall the three families got together at a central location, the Cleveland area, for two days to discuss the idea and find out how serious they really were. The were surprised to find how much they agreed on the basic concept. "We were concerned that the Brethren weren't being active enough in home missions," Dick says. "We really need to work at spreading the gospel here! There's a big part of this country we haven't touched. People need more than what traditional or fundamentalist churches offer. They get you so far, but don't really move you into a deep community of faith. That's the biblical understanding of faith. Brethren need to stop apologizing for who they are and go and preach it and live it and invite others to it boldly and not be afraid to go into new areas. We didn't know about new church development in the past. We had no background. We didn't think of those words 'new church development.' We just thought of going somewhere and starting a

The three pastors being considered were not announced. This was done for two reasons. First, Stanley Earhart and the three men felt that the project idea had to stand on its own. Secondly, each man had a pastorate and could not discuss leaving until the project was approved. The discussion was thorough and encouraging, but it snagged on this secrecy. The board members wanted to know who would be sent to Vermont. One of the board members, who was a leader of the BRF, criticized the project saying that it was going to be a "lifestyle" church while the Brethren in Maine were interested in salvation. Dick, who was a member of the board, remembers wanting to leap to his feet and rebut that accusation.

When the board broke for lunch, Dick took a walk to think over what to do. He had Dennis and Paul's permission to reveal their identities if necessary. When the meeting reconvened, he stood up and announced who it was that would go. There was a sigh of relief. Dennis and Dick were well-respected in the district. The board approved the proposal. Stanley enjoined the board to secrecy. District conference still had to vote on the project. Until then the churches of the three pastors could not be told.

Events began to move quickly. A specially called district conference was scheduled for June 15. August was set as a target date for beginning in Vermont. Because of this schedule, the three families were forced to make plans before the final decision. They all traveled to the Brattleboro area in early June to look for places to live. There had been a time in the early days of the dream that communal living had been considered. The men were more sanguine about this than the women. "When the guys were first talking about this, they tended to be very romantic," Dorothy Grout remembers. "We could all live together and everything would be fine! We wives tended to to be much more practical about the whole thing. We were adamant that we would have to have separate living quarters. The guys would all agree with us now."

They found a large, somewhat run-down clapboard house a few miles from the village of Putney and about nine miles from Brattleboro. It sat on a three-acre lot and looked out over the Vermont mountains. It was large enough to divide into three good-sized apartments. They made an offer, subject to a favorable district conference decision.

When it came on June 15, 1981, the decision was unanimous. "People were crying," Paul Grout remembers. "It was the most conservative people in the district and the most liberal. There was an incredible feeling!" Dick says, "We felt overwhelmingly strong support, even from the plain people. They were mostly supporting the Maine project financially but really gave us spiritual support and encouragement. One plain brother was impressed that we were asking for only one-third of a salary each. The free ministry idea appealed."

There were only two months to make the announcements to their congregations, finish their work, get financing for the house, say all the good-byes, and get ready to move. It was a hectic time. Finally, August 17, 1981 found the Coffmans and Shreckhises arriving at their new home. The Grouts came one week later.

In every previous pastoral assignment the families had been greeted by eager parishioners. In Vermont, no one took note of their arrival. "Nobody was here with warm soup on the table," Pat Shreckhise says. They had to move in and get settled alone. This was a more discouraging task than they had expected. The house was in bad shape. It needed work not only to divide it up, but to make it livable. Contrary to the purchase agreement they thought they had negotiated, the appliances had not been left in the house. The first few months were spent in fixing up the house, beginning to get acquainted with the community, and simply establishing themselves. As they did this, they told people why they had come. They began to visit churches in the area. They also began to look for part-time work. Their first jobs were in the apple harvest.

People were friendly but reserved. Were these people a new cult? Were they hippies living in a commune? Were they fanatics intent on converting people with high pressure evangelism? The residents were not afraid nor discourteous. That part of New England had many strange people coming and going, people from the eastern metropolitan areas, and the inhabitants were tolerant of peculiarities. Even the "old Vermonters," of whom there are not many left, were used to these peregrinations. The attitude was wait-and-see. Two things did impress people right off. One was that seminary-trained pastors were willing to do menial work. The other was that they were fixing up their real estate. Both these things spoke of self-reliance and responsibility.

The task of any pastor/developer is hard. On top of everything else that normally has to be done, the three pastors had to get jobs and fix up the house while their families had to live on top of each other in the parts of the house fit for occupancy. All this had to be done without the kind of moral support that would have come to the pastor of a new congregation near other Churches of the Brethren and far from the district office. Their support had to come across hundreds of miles from Pennsylvania. But it did come. People came up to work on the house. A remodeling fund was set up. This help was obviously heartening to the Brethren in Vermont, but it was also good for the district and gave many people an opportunity to get involved in the venture.

Though their time was absorbed by the necessities of living, Dick, Dennis, and Paul managed to begin to visit people in the community. They began to look for a place to hold their first public worship. They found a large, ornately trimmed wooden house called Solar Hill on the outskirts of Brattleboro. There was meeting space on the main floor above which were apartments. There, on December 13, 1981, they worshiped publicly for the first time. But they set January 3, 1982 for the first officially announced worship. An ad was placed in the paper. On that day the Church of the Brethren opened its door in Vermont. Two people came in addition to the six adults and six children of the three families—14 people in all.

The Vermont "missioners," as they sometimes call themselves, were not discouraged. They expected the project to be a long, hard pull. They were concerned first off not with attendance but with developing a network of friendships and relationships. Let people get to know them. Serve the community. Get involved. Slowly invite people. Don't push. This was their mission approach. They knew they had something to share. As they got to know the community, they became more sure of this. But let the project grow naturally. Learn as well as teach. Receive as well as give. Live with the people. Don't try to change them. Let that happen in a different way. Paul Grout says, "I don't think any of us are uncomfortable being with people who may have a totally different moral pattern than we do. We believe Christ is going to change it, and it's not going to be us. It'd just be terrible to come in here and say, 'You have to do this and this so that you can be part of us.'"

As they settled in, they began to get more permanent jobs: Dorothy as an elementary school teacher; Reba in a nursing home; Paul as a part-time art teacher; Dennis as a dishwasher in a senior center and as volunteer director of an emergency shelter for the homeless; Dick as a part-time department store janitor. They courted other ministers in the area, joined the ministers association, helped them organize their events, sought out local peace groups, were the subject of several articles in the Brattleboro paper. On April 11, they held an Easter sunrise service on the hillside across from the home, which they now called Brethren House. Twenty-eight people attended. There was a breakfast following the service. "People just stayed and stayed," the business meeting minutes of April 14 note. "The fellowship was great. Needless to say, we all felt very good about this kind of involvement."

The meeting place at Solar Hill became less and less acceptable because of noise and interruptions from the occupants. It was too far from Brethren House, and the people showing interest were closer to Putney than Brattleboro. Early in May the fledgling fellowship arranged to rent a room for worship in the Putney Central School. On May 26, the fellowship settled on a name for itself—the Genesis Church of the Brethren, taking as their basis not the Old Testament use of this Greek word for beginning but the New Testament application from the first chapter of the Gospel of John. By mid-1982, the Genesis church had made many friends, and a few people were beginning to think about getting involved.

Among the people who came to the Genesis church during that first half year were the Busbys. Bill, a research scientist at the Massachusetts Institute of Technology, Helen, a psychologist, and Billie Jr., their 15-year-old son, live in Sterling, Massachusetts, about an hour from Boston. Helen, who grew up in Rhode Island as a Unitarian/Universalist, has a sister who lives in eastern Pennsylvania. Helen experienced a conversion in an American Baptist congregation in Massachusetts. When she told her sister she was planning to be baptized, she was astonished to find out that her sister had become an active member of the Indian Creek Church of the Brethren in Harleysville, Pennsylvania, north of Philadelphia. Her sister began to send Helen *A Guide for Biblical Studies*, "telling me about these Brethren things she liked so very much." On a visit to Pennsylvania the following spring, Bill and Helen were invited to attend love feast. The love feast was very appealing. Helen found a combination of qualities in the Brethren that fit her understanding and experience.

"I think the most attractive aspect," Helen says, "was the attempt to live out the gospel without denying the central tenets of faith. In my experience as a Unitarian/Universalist, there was a social liberality that seemed to necessitate dropping the spiritual, dropping the gospel. Having come to Christianity in a conversion experience, I felt that was too important to leave out. Without the Brethren we wouldn't have found a denomination that we felt wedded the two. It seems that people are either on one side or the other. In spite of the enormous diversity and differences of opinion [among the Brethren], there is a body of believers that attempts to live this out in such a unique way."

Helen and Bill joined the Church of the Brethren at Indian Creek even though it is hundreds of miles from their home. They came down as often as possible, especially for love feasts. Impressed with their faith and their enthusiasm for the church, Luke Brandt, pastor at Indian Creek, made it his project to contact scattered Brethren in the greater Boston area and to try to gather together a Boston area fellowship. This group began to meet at regular intervals.

It is difficult to start a church with Brethren scattered throughout a metropolitan area. They are widely separated; they have often joined other churches; sometimes they are glad to be away from other Brethren. "I personally felt that the Boston fellowship was not getting off the ground, at least not at a rate which I felt necessary for my own spiritual growth," Bill Busby says. "I just didn't feel that I could wait around, and I didn't see anything that I could personally do which would accelerate this process."

The Boston group had heard of the Brattleboro project and knew there were three ministers there. They had discussed asking one of them to come down to Boston from time to time. "I think just out of desperation one day I took a road map and said, 'Where is Brattleboro anyway?' I was amazed to find that it was literally just a few miles across the Massachusetts border," Bill says. "We actually calculated the mileage. It was as far to go from our house to Brattleboro as it had been to go from our house to the meeting place that we used in the Boston area in Pembroke on the south shore."

Helen called Brethren House and asked if the Busbys could come to the love feast on Maundy Thursday. "I expected to find what I in fact did find," Bill recalls, "spiritually alive people who are willing to go out on a limb and move to a new area and do the things necessary to start a new fellowship." Helen's expectations were confirmed too. "The Indian Creek congregation was my only contact with the Brethren other than reading Brethren history books, so my contact with the Brethren was very idealized. The Indian Creek congregation was very warm, accepting, extremely friendly. You felt as though you were a brother or sister in the faith immediately, whether they had ever set eyes on you before or not. I brought that expectation here. I just knew they would be the same type of Brethren. And they were!"

The Busbys believe there are many others in New England who would find a home with the Brethren. "There is a real need, a real spiritual hunger, in many of the people I know," Bill says, "but they can't come to terms with the more conservatively oriented, fundamentalist type of churches that they have come into contact with."

Debbie and Adam Wetzel were one of the first families to reach out to the Vermont missioners. They offered their home as a meeting place. They have invited friends in for coffee to meet them and hear about the plans for the church. They helped persuade them to move their worship services to Putney. Debbie was the first person to join in the planning and responsibility for the new fellowship. Adam and Debbie operate a small business producing and selling gift and specialty items crafted from wood and slate. "What I like about the church is the worship services," Debbie says. "There is something different every Sunday. In some churches everything is the same. But I go there on Sunday mornings and it's more of a worship experience. There's something to think about. There is not so much ceremony. It's more spontaneous." Adam, who came from a Lutheran background and likes more liturgy in the service comments on the qualities the three families bring to the community. "They have a basic innocence about them. I mean, they know what's going on and everything, but it's just that their whole spirit is childlike innocence, and it shows. That's really beautiful."

The Robinsons, Donnie and Ann, were also one of the first families to take the Genesis Brethren in. They became friends first with the Coffmans and then with the whole fellowship. Now they have become active participants. They had looked for a long time for a church that fit them. What they like about the Brethren is the belief in simplicity of life, the emphasis on the family, and the sense of community. "I'm just very happy that we got involved with the Brethren," Donnie says. "Maybe our prayers were answered and God led us to them. We feel like we're coming home finally."

Commitment comes slowly in Vermont. There is a spirit of tolerance that says in effect: We're glad you're here. We're glad you can come up here and do your own thing. You go right ahead and do your thing, and we'll do ours. In a developing community with new subdivisions, the people move in to get ahead. Their object is not to draw back from society but to establish their place in it. For many, joining a church is a natural part of putting down roots. In southern

Vermont, people are not trying to get ahead. They are trying to back up. Their object is not to make a place for themselves in society but to get away from the rat race and build a different life for themselves. Church tends to be associated with the conventional life they are trying to get away from. Commitment tends to look like acquiescence.

Many of the people in southern Vermont are looking for a simpler life. There is a strong peace movement there. People want to find genuine community. These are the values of the Genesis Brethren, so they fit in well. But they want to say that real life and peace and community come from Christ, that without him there is an emptiness at the center of the search. They think they see this emptiness in the casual relationships, the anything-is-okay-as-long-as-it-doesn't-hurt-somebody attitude. They see people who in the sixties and early seventies made commitments to movements that failed. They see people of conviction who are disappointed and distrustful, determined not to be taken in. Their task is not to find people looking for a church home but to invite wary, battle-weary people into a home they no longer believe exists.

The Genesis Brethren have what it takes to do that. They combine peace concerns and social activism with spiritual renewal. They lift up the example of Christ but also proclaim his presence. Paul Grout says, "I think we've talked a lot in the Church of the Brethren about example—the Sermon on the Mount—and so often our center has been exclusively there. Being in Christ means living up to the teachings. That's part of it, but there is also a living presence, a now relationship, a touch to the Holy Spirit with Christ. Following the teachings is key, but that presence actually lives."

In September 1983, the Genesis church was given fellowship status by the Southern Pennsylvania district. At the beginning of 1984, it has a membership of 20 and attendance of 35 to 40. It is growing slowly, feeling its way in a strange land. "I see more and more people coming to us and finding meaning," Paul Grout says. "I say more and more not for numbers. We're not into the thing where we have to have a lot of numbers to justify ourselves, but we came here to minister to people. And we came here to help people." Here his voice softens and tears come to his eyes. "And we came here to bring Christ alive to people. My vision is seeing people relating to us for whom Christ is coming alive and who are coming alive within the body which is our group."

The year 1981 saw the most new church development activity to date, three new starts. It also saw two more projects that were not in a strict sense new but were instances where new energy and commitment transformed something already in existence.

For many years the Church of the Brethren in Oakland, California was regarded as a dying church. The neighborhood had changed; people had moved away; its membership was small; and the large, old church building was a burden. In 1978 the congregation decided to look beyond its struggle to survive and try something new. It created the Greater Bay Area Fellowship (GBAF) in order to draw together the Brethren scattered throughout the heavily populated San Francisco Bay area. The Pacific Southwest Conference (In that district the word "conference" is used in place of "district.") agreed to provide funds to help underwrite the idea. Fumitaka Matsuoka, Japanese-born Brethren minister, was called to be pastor. The plan was to continue services at the Oakland church, but to hold house church meetings twice a month in various homes throughout the bay area. When Matsu (as Fumitaka Matsuoka is called) arrived in the fall of 1978, several meetings had already been held.

In October the program was properly launched, and for a time there was enthusiasm. Six new families plus some Oakland families became active. Sometimes as many as 50 people attended. There were usually 25 to 30. But this group was not able to attract new participants. People who did not have Brethren ties would visit as guests but would not return. Toward the end of 1980 Matsu realized the GBAF was not going to become anything more than the occasional gathering that it was.

At the church retreat in the spring of 1981, Matsu brought an analysis of the Oakland/GBAF project with four possible options. One of them was to shift the focus from Oakland and the GBAF and find a site where a new church could be started. The congregation agreed to this option. Both the Pacific Southwest Conference and the General Board agreed to support this new direction.

The city of Fremont was selected. It is centrally located for the people from Oakland in the north and the GBAF people in San Jose and the extreme south bay area. Whenever the GBAF had met in Fremont, it had had its largest attendance. Fremont is a fast-growing area. Though home prices are high throughout the bay area, they are lower in Fremont than in other places. One of the most active families in GBAF lived in Fremont. A number of active Oakland families committed themselves to make the long trip down to Fremont.

The congregation surveyed the community, writing to 100 people with and without Brethren background. They received nine positive responses. Adding those to the people already committed, they felt they had enough people to begin. Services would be discontinued at Oakland, except for once a month; the building would be rented. A meeting place was found at the Fremont Community Center, which is surrounded by a park and near a small lake. In effect one congregation would end and another would begin.

On December 6, 1981, the first worship service was held in the new Fremont quarters. The response was discouraging. Only 36 people came. Of the nine positive respondents to the survey, only one couple came. As the group continued to meet, the GBAF people attended occasionally, but gradually dropped out. The people at Oakland who had actively opposed the move dropped away. The only regular people were the Oakland faithful and a few core GBAF people. For a while it appeared that the move had effectively destroyed what little life had existed in Oakland and the GBAF as separate groups and had not replaced it with new life.

The congregation passed out 3,000 fliers and got four responses. Matsu knocked on doors, but people were suspicious of him because of his Asian features, associating him with the "Moonies." It was hard for him to dispel these suspicions. Very few of the hoped-for Brethren from the area were attracted. This pattern of effort and failure continued for several months. The district leaders and Merle Crouse began to question the project as did Matsu and the congregation. Had they planned poorly? Was Matsu, who is academically inclined and has a doctorate in theology and philosophy of religion, the wrong person for the job?

But in 1982, new people slowly began to come. A few of them were of Brethren background. One couple moved into the area from a large Church of the Brethren in the east. But what was most important was that some of the people were from the community and did not have Brethren ties. They wanted what this church had to offer. Attendance began to pick up into the 35-40 range. In the fall of 1982 a name was chosen, Fellowship in Christ Church of the Brethren. That same fall a Sunday school was developed and some excellent adult classes were offered. The fellowship time on Sunday morning was lengthened and emphasized. The Oakland people, for the first time in years, began to feel that they were part of something that was growing. The conflicts and tensions that had existed in the old church were gone because the people who had been embroiled in them had left. "This life here in Fremont is so different in contrast to the Oakland time," Matsu says. "For the first time they can say they really enjoy the church. At Oakland they came to the church out of their dedication, out of their commitment, not because they really enjoyed and appreciated it so much."

The Fellowship in Christ church has not yet proven fully that it can survive in Fremont. But there is good reason for hope. That it exists and has grown at all is a surprise. It is forming a new church out of two things that do not ordinarily make for church development--a dying church that most people had given up on and an informal group of Brethren scattered over a large metropolitan area. But in a sense, it isn't really making a church out of these but is making something new. Maybe the old congregation and the GBAF had to die for this to happen. The Fremont church is not a continuation of those two groups but a new creation. Until it began to have its own identity and attract new people, it had no real life of its own. That this resurrection is indeed following that death is a credit to the faith of the old Oakland core, to the commitment of a few GBAF members, and to the quiet, steady leadership of Matsu.

At the beginning of 1984, Fellowship in Christ church has 46 members and an attendance of 40. It continues the GBAF meetings once a month for some families in the San Jose area who want to keep in touch. In March, 1983, Wayne Fralin, a lay person from Florida who does feasibility studies for the banking industry, studied the Fremont area and made recommendations for their future building plans. Land prices and constructions costs are very high. It will be some time before the congregation will have a permanent home, and then it may have to be something other than a new building. Surprisingly, a small core of interest in the Brethren is also developing in the Berkeley area, back up north near Oakland.

At present, the future of the Brethren in the bay area is uncertain. The only other congregation, the San Francisco church, is small and diminishing in membership. The spark of new activity at Fremont is the first real sign of new life for the Brethren in the bay area.

The other 1981 old/new church development project is the only completely rural project. Its history goes back further than that of any other project, and it is the first project in what promises to be one of the most fertile fields for new church development in the Church of the Brethren.

As early as 1966, Don Fike, pastor of the Castañer Church of the Brethren in Puerto Rico, began to go up into the mountains in the Lares area to a small village called Río Prieto, running along the top of a ridge. In 1968 a small group (12-20) began to gather in homes on Sunday afternoons for worship. These meetings continued when Guillermo Encarnación became pastor in 1972. In 1978 the group acquired a run-down building for its use. This building is owned by the leader of a spiritualist group, now defunct, and its use was given to the Río Prieto Brethren in exchange for their promise to remodel it and also allow it to be used for a health clinic.

Late in 1980, Beth and Keith Nonemaker, two recent seminary graduates, went to Puerto Rico as volunteers and served the Río Prieto group as their first full-time leaders. In October 1981, the district of Florida and Puerto Rico, recognized Río Prieto as a fellowship. After more than a decade as a preaching point of the Castañer church, this small group of farmers and farmworkers took the first step toward becoming a church in its own right. Both the district and the General Board made a commitment to help support the church so that it would continue to have a pastoral program.

Keith and Beth trained Sunday school teachers; taught Bible studies; gave preaching instruction to the members who served as lay leaders; held youth meetings; gave instruction in church history, the peace position, Brethren heritage, and Brethren practices; and involved new people in the church. They baptized nine people. They enjoyed their work and stayed several months past the end of their term. Eventually they returned to the States to take up pastoral work there. For a time the church was without leadership, but in the fall of 1982, Mario and Olga Serrano were called by the Castañer congregation—Mario to pastor Castaner and Olga to be part-time pastor at Río Prieto.

There are about ten families in the congregation, but there is one large family that forms its nucleus, the family of Luís Perez. Luigi (as he is known) owns and operates a 20-acre coffee farm where he also grows oranges, bananas, and other fruits and vegetables. Luigi has been the patriarch and lay spiritual leader of the church, the person who has kept the small fellowship alive over the years. Today the membership is 24 and attendance is 43.

"They are very dynamic," Merle Crouse says. "There are lots of children and young people. There is no other church up there. It is the community church. It is the rallying place for that whole community. It's going to give that whole community a new personality. Being faithful evangelicals is the key thing, as it is in all the Puerto Rican churches. There, evangelical means you are a non-Catholic Christian. Your focus is on Bible study, fellowship, and very active, participatory worship."

The Río Prieto Brethren are hidden in the beautiful mountains of Puerto Rico. They worship in a remodeled meetinghouse that looks out over a breathtaking vista, far from stateside Brethren. Yet they love the Church of the Brethren and have a vision for the church. "In Puerto Rico there are many evangelical churches, even rich ones," says Luigi, "but they don't do anything to help the poor people. The important thing is to start churches whose goal is to better the spiritual condition and also the physical and material condition. We also need to have ministers and missionaries prepared bilingually. It's very important that the Church of the Brethren progresses and grows in Puerto Rico."

Thus the last five months of 1981 were a pivotal time: three new congregations were started; one was created through recognition; and one started over. Four of the five were unusual in some way; two were experimental; one reaffirmed the effectiveness of the basic new church model. Before August, 1981, new church development moved slowly. After December, 1981, it continued at a heightened pace and with increased variety.

CHAPTER THREE
GAINING MOMENTUM

In January, 1982 the district of Oregon and Washington and the General Board began to support a small Hispanic group in Tonasket, Washington. The roots of this project went back to August, 1979 and the stabbing murder of a migrant worker in the orchard of Jim and Sonya Rothrock, members of the Ellisforde Church of the Brethren. In October of that year, the Rothrocks and others concerned about the Hispanics formed Para Todos Latinos Ministries (PTLM). At harvest time and then again the next year, PTLM brought Spanish-speaking evangelists to preach in the community. But the PTLM leaders believed that a permanent ministry was needed; and in September of 1981, at their request, Raul Martinez, a minister of Mexican background, began to gather a small congregation. The Ellisforde church helped to support him, as did the Free Methodists and a new, small, independent group called Living Light Fellowship; but more money was needed.

Both the district leadership and Merle Crouse felt this was a project worth supporting. They knew it was risky. They were not sure there were enough people, either permanent residents or migrants, to support a Hispanic ministry. They did not know which denomination, if any, it would affiliate with. But they felt it was a sincere effort and deserved a chance, so they committed both district and General Board funds.

The group did not thrive. There are various views as to why. One is that the permanent residents did not respond, and although the migrants did, they were mostly illegal aliens, always coming and going. It was thus hard to establish a permanent fellowship. Another view has it that the local Brethren were willing to support the project with money but did not get involved directly. By district request the General Board money stopped at the end of 1982, and early in 1983 the district support ended. Raul Martinez continues the ministry on a reduced scale while working at another job. His ministry continues to be supported by the Living Light Fellowship.

Only a few weeks after the Tonasket support began, on February 28, 1982, a new congregation in the district of Illinois and Wisconsin met for the first time. The place was a high-ceilinged gymnasium in an elementary school in a new subdivision of Carol Stream, Illinois, a far western suburb of Chicago. There, surrounded by banners put up to soften the harsh gym atmosphere, 107 people gathered, many of them visitors from other churches in the district.

The beginning of this fellowship can be traced back to 1977 when Howard Royer and Doreen Myers, members of the Highland Avenue Church of the Brethren in Elgin, began to talk in the witness commission about starting new churches. Their concern was taken to district board by Carl Myers, district executive and husband of Doreen. Ozzie Goering, the board chairperson, was also interested in new churches. At the next meeting, action was taken that resulted in the creation of a new church development task force.

Early in 1978 this group began to meet, and for the next two years they carried on an active and fertile investigation. They considered at least eight different groups or sites. They gave some financial support to at least four groups. Most of these were experimental and were initiated by people who came to the task force for support. Finally, after much thought and after consultation with Merle Crouse, the task force decided to focus on one carefully planned project following the basic new church model used at Blacksburg.

Don Robinson did a feasibility study; and basing their decision on that study, the task force selected Carol Stream. When the site selection process and their fund-raising campaign were well underway, they called Don Leiter to be the pastor/developer. Don had been pastor of one of those new churches in the early sixties, Immanuel Church in Paoli, Pennsylvania. There is a second link to that earlier new church movement in Judd Peter, chairperson of the task force and a longtime member of the Boulder Hill church near Aurora. Judd first joined the Church of the Brethren in the Boulder Hill congregation in 1961, just a few years after it was started in the new housing development where he lived. Judd is convinced that the Church of the Brethren has something to offer, and he has been the spearhead of the Carol Stream project. While it is still a fellowship, he serves as its moderator.

Don Leiter accepted the call and began work August 1, 1981. Like Norman Harsh he attended a Lutheran workshop, and through the fall and into the winter he knocked on more than 2,100 doors. The name Christ Church of the Brethren was chosen for the group. By the end of February, the preliminary work was completed, and a group of interested families were ready to begin worship.

Christ church has attracted a core group of mostly young married couples with small children. Some have come from two nearby Brethren churches; some have come from Catholic backgrounds; some from fundamentalist experiences. In discussing the new group, Dale Minnich, who came from the Highland Avenue church in Elgin, says, "One of the things that I think really is a strength is that we have a group of people from very varied backgrounds, but who are really sincere in seeking God's leading in their lives. And the answers aren't always the same for everybody, but the search I think is something that we really do have in common. We don't seem to have the people who are just very casual, non-involved participants. There really is a search there."

"I think that's true," agrees Chip Flag. "I think that's what maybe helps bring all the differences together. Most of the people who are here don't just want to form a religious organization. They want to reform themselves. They don't just want to build up a certain kind of church or something." And Dennis Davidson adds, "If you want to be a spectator, this isn't the place to go!"

Daryl Gabel, who was elected church board chairperson, talks about what is special about the church, "I think our congregation has been abundantly blessed with God's ministry of healing." He describes the healing of a child with a hip deformity. "It was just obvious to me and to the whole congregation that we were a real part of God's hand in that particular case. I've seen blessings poured out and miracles performed in the lives of others. I feel there is a special movement, a special spirit present with us."

A special time for June Davidson was love feast. "I went into that with real hesitation because it was something very different, but through the music and those bonds that we'd already built and being together and being quiet and reevaluating, it was just beautiful."

"Christ church has its own being," Don Leiter says, "which is another significant thing about the Church of the Brethren. You don't have to fit into anybody's mold. You can create your own community of believers and be truly part of the church. It's the importance of Christian community over Christian doctrine. The chief evidence is response to people rather than 'Do you believe exactly the right way?'"

Not everything about Christ church has developed smoothly. The fund-raising campaign did not net as much money as hoped. The site, which was purchased late in 1981, cost more than anticipated. Attendance and membership have grown more slowly than Don and the task force would like. As 1984 begins and they approach their second anniversary, there are 19 members and an average attendance of 35.

When a church is begun with a full-time pastor and with the expectation of a building within several years, there is economic pressure to grow. Often in the second year there is a period of slowed growth, and then that pressure becomes more intense. Christ church is just finishing its second year. The members of a new church have to separate economic criteria from spiritual criteria as they judge their church. "By my evaluative analysis, this is developing very slowly," Don says. "I just get very impatient with it. But at the same time, there are times like the last four Tuesday night meetings where people were sharing out of their faith journey—where they've come from and how they are here in the Christ Church of the Brethren and what that is meaning in their lives today. There's no question about the need for and the validity of the church here."

On March 20, 1982, less than a month after Christ church began to meet in Illinois, a new fellowship gathered for the first time in a carport in Vega Baja, Puerto Rico. There were eight adults and four children. The pastor, Jaime Rivera, notes that those first eight were like the Schwarzenau eight who founded the Church of the Brethren. The roots of this church go back to Jaime's childhood in Castañer, where he was born in 1940.

When he was six, Jaime and others in his family were treated for a blood disease at the hospital in Castañer operated by the Church of the Brethren. That was his first contact with the Brethren. Later, as a young man, he joined the congregation that grew out of this Brethren service work. In 1964 he moved to the San Juan metropolitan area where he took a job with Warner-Lambert, got married, started a family, and began night classes at Ward University. During these years he became active in the Church of God (based in Cleveland, Tennessee), becoming president of his congregation's Sunday school. Between 1977 and 1980, he studied nights at the Church of God seminary to increase his knowledge of the Bible and to grow in his faith.

In 1975 he and his family moved into a new subdivision in Vega Baja, which is on the outer ring of the San Juan metropolitan district, just three miles from the Atlantic coast. In this development and in Residencial el Rosario which is next to it, there are now 1500 homes and more are being built. They are pleasant, flat-roofed, white stucco houses with arched porch arcades and carved wooden doors. They are neatly painted and surrounded by low stucco walls or iron fences with the arched gates and ornate grillwork seen all over Puerto Rico. These developments are thriving communities with many young families and children and with only one other church.

Jaime saw that this was a good place to start a new congregation. He approached the Church of God leaders with the idea. By this time his ministerial abilities had been recognized; but instead of encouraging him in his plan, they asked him to serve a tiny group in another village. Jaime felt that this group had no future; there were too few people and too many churches in the area. He tried again to persuade the Church of God leadership to support a church in Residencial el Rosario. "I saw that the harvest is here," he says. "It's a new place. It's a new people. It's younger people. It's the proper place! Where the people are, you have to go! That's the message of the New Testament in the book of Acts. Paul moved where the people were. To Corinth —a large city. Because the people were there. That's the vision!"

In 1981, the pulpit at the Castañer church was empty because of a pastoral change. Jaime's brother, Jorge Rivera, was moderator of the church at that time, and Jorge's wife asked Jaime to come and preach. Jaime preached several times and also gave a seminar for Sunday school teachers. This put him back in touch with the Brethren, and he told them of his vision for Vega Baja and asked if the Church of the Brethren could help. In mid-1981, Jorge carried a letter from Jaime to the district board of Florida/Puerto Rico explaining his idea and asking for support. Already in 1980 Jaime had found a small lot on a street corner near one of the entrances to the Residencial el Rosario. It was ideal for the church, too good to pass up. Jaime took a risk and without any backing promised the owner he would buy the land.

The district of Florida/Puerto Rico had been planning to start a new congregation in Puerto Rico. When Jaime's letter arrived, they were looking at Ponce, almost directly south of Vega Baja on the Caribbean Coast. The Ponce project was not moving as hoped, and Jaime's project interested the district people. In January, 1982, four people representing the district went to visit Vega Baja. They liked what they saw.

The district already had $120,000 committed to the Ponce project. This money was to come from the Shenandoah district in Virginia. Shenandoah has a small area with many churches. The people in the district wanted to be in new church development but did not think their area needed more Churches of the Brethren. Thus Shenandoah had resources but no field. Florida/Puerto Rico had a large field but only limited resources. The two districts had made an agreement that Shenandoah would help finance the Ponce project. Now with that project on hold, they switched their consideration to Vega Baja.

Jaime knew from his brother Jorge that district sponsorship was a possibility. But he felt a sense of urgency. It was time to start. He went to the Church of God leaders at the end of 1981 and told them he was leaving the church. He stood up in his congregation and said good-by. He was careful not to invite people to follow him. He did not want to take members away from the Church of God. His calling was to start a new church with new members, not to split people off from the Church of God. (He says he has since kept a good relationship with the Church of God pastor in the area.)

Jaime spent three months in preparation; and on March 20, 1982, the first group of worshipers of what would become Iglesia de los Hermanos Cristo el Señor (Christ the Lord Church of the Brethren) gathered in the carport of Jorge Toledo, several blocks from Jaime's home. There was still no word from the Brethren. "If the church accepted it or didn't accept it, my decision was to go," Jaime says. "I knew God was with me, and he would open one door, either the Brethren or some other door. He would do it! There was a feeling in my spirit that they would accept it. Maybe there would be trouble, but they would finally accept it. I had security from the Holy Spirit. The door is here."

Jaime's feeling was right. The Florida/Puerto Rico Brethren did accept the project, and in October of 1982 at district conference, they gave it fellowship status. The purchase of the lot was completed and a large sign was put on the corner to announce the new church. For a year the group continued to meet in the carport, but by the spring of 1983, they needed more space. The Shenandoah district purchased a large tent for them, and in April they put it up on their lot. This will be their home until their building is built. Don Horne, an architect from the Elk Run congregation in Shenandoah district, volunteered to draw the plans, and the district paid his expenses. The plans have been completed, and the laying of the cornerstone is scheduled for April, 1984. At the end of 1983, there were 31 members and an average attendance of 50. Jorge Toledo, also a former Church of God lay preacher, serves as assistant pastor. Both Jaime and Jorge are free ministers, each working full-time in responsible positions for Warner-Lambert. Jaime is in management and has an excellent salary and good opportunity for advancement, but he feels his calling is to be a pastor, and he looks forward to being in the ministry full-time. Jorge Toledo is a powerful preacher and among the Brethren in Puerto Rico is in demand as an evangelist.

To get started in the community, Jaime has designed a survey questionnaire, and people in the congregation are taking it door-to-door. The goal is not to persuade people to join the church but to find out what the community needs. One of Jaime's dreams is to start an elementary school in the neighborhood. While Jaime and Jorge were still in the Church of God, they helped start a mission in the Dominican Republic. Jorge was one of the leaders of this effort, which the Vega Baja fellowship continues to support. Several times a year members go there to preach and witness. They have helped to build a church building at the mission. The project is in a place called Biajama and is larger than the parent Vega Baja group. It symbolizes their large dreams.

The Vega Baja people are almost all young. The have many small children. When they worship, they use guitars, maracas, and güiros (a serrated gourd, played by rubbing a stick along its surface), and they have a powerful amplifier that can be heard all over the neighborhood. They are fervent in prayer. They talk about love and inner peace. Religion is a matter of the heart. They are warm, demonstrative people. They hug one another. They are not as reserved as stateside Brethren. They stress the personal presence of Jesus. "I didn't join a religion," Jaime says. "I joined a person. I joined Jesus. I am part of Jesus, part of his body. I work for his body."

This is Puerto Rican Christianity; it has a strong Pentecostal flavor. Yet, here is what Jaime says about being Brethren in Puerto

Rico, "We are peacemakers because this came from the Bible. We have the feetwashing. I open the Bible and teach that we believe you have to respect others. No force in religion. I teach them [people in the congregation] to do some social work, encourage them to help in the neighborhood—help others, share the love. To be a Christian is a way of life. It's not to talk one religion; it's not to say, 'It will make you better than others to be Brethren—if you just hold this religion.' No! You get the sectarian barrier there. Accept others are they are, but share the love. Show that Jesus lives in your heart, and share that love with others. I believe the Brethren have that kind of right doctrine, and I teach that way."

On the same day that Cristo el Señor church met for the first time, Bob and Martie Kaufman, volunteers from Michigan, arrived on Culebra, a small island east of Puerto Rico. Here for many years U.S. Navy jets, flying from the main island, held target practice. Along one of the lovely white beaches a battered tank still rusts in the sun. When the Navy finally abandoned the island, it had few community services, no prospects for development, and no real identity or sense of community. It was a run-down, forsaken place. A doctor from the island who had worked briefly at Castañer hospital contacted the Brethren in the hope that they might start a service project on Culebra.

Phyllis Carter, then Florida/Puerto Rico district executive, and Merle Crouse saw an opportunity to try something on Culebra called a base Christian community, a model from the Latin American Catholic church. This is a synthesis of Bible study, worship, and community action. People commit themselves to each other to identify their needs, work together to meet the needs, and worship together to sustain one another. It is not a church as we think of it, nor is it a political action group of the sort we have. It is a combination of both, a form of Christian community arising in Latin American where people are powerless. Culebra seemed like a place where a base Christian community might grow. Bob and Martie were seasoned volunteers who had served in a Mennonite program in Kenya for three years before returning to the states to take jobs as social workers. Now they wanted to go back into overseas volunteer work.

The project on Culebra has gone slowly. Residents were suspicious at first. Who were these people? Why didn't they have jobs? Who was supporting them? Culebra is midway between Puerto Rico and the U.S. Virgin Islands on one of the routes followed by pleasure seekers in the Caribbean. Were these people beach bums or drifters just passing through? Slowly the Kaufmans found things they could do. Bob, who has mechanical ability, discovered that there are no repair shops on the island where appliances can be fixed. When they break down, they are discarded. He began a repair service. The island has no fresh water and must either ship it from the main island or process sea water. There is a desalinization plant which rarely works. Bob began to work on getting it fixed. The day care center/preschool was about to close; Martie and Bob volunteered to work there and help keep it open. Martie started a small service baking bread and selling it at cost. All the while they looked for a way to get people involved in longer term community development.

It has become apparent that their skills lie in community development. The plan for creating a base Christian community has been dropped by the district. Bob and Martie continue to serve the people of Culebra as community service workers. The future of the Culebra project is uncertain.

While these projects were developing in the early months of 1982, something was formed at the Brotherhood level that underlined the increasing importance and reach of new church development. In January the General Board staff met in retreat with the district executives. In that meeting a strong recommendation was made to Merle Crouse that a new church development coordinating committee be established to advise him. People were beginning to take new church development seriously. It was growing like topsy. It was felt that Merle needed help to reflect on it, to decide where the money should go, to develop leadership, and to interpret and explain the movement throughout the denomination. On April 25, the committee was formed with four members. In June it met again and three more were added. There are two district executives, two lay members of district church development committees, a pastor of one of the new churches, Merle, and a second General Board staff member.

The majority of the new church projects proceed cautiously, guided by feasibility studies and careful planning, but Merle and others have been willing to experiment. Culebra was one instance. Two other projects developed in 1982 that took Brethren in new directions. The Antelope Park Church of the Brethren in Lincoln, Nebraska, has had a history of helping refugees. In 1981 Mary Frazier, whose husband Glenn was pastor of the Antelope Park church, worked for an agency that resettled refugees. As Khmer refugees fleeing from Kampuchea (Cambodia) came to Lincoln, they showed interest in the Antelope Park church; and the congregation decided to begin ministering to them. In a matter of only months, the stream of refugees turned into a flood. The church became a center for the Khmer community. Sunday morning attendance rose from an average of 100 to 188. Suddenly this small, stable congregation was being swallowed up by a wave of people new to the U.S., new to Lincoln, and many of them new to Christianity.

The church made a decision that its ministry was to be a spiritual ministry as well as a social and material ministry. Because the Khmer group was almost as large as the original congregation and because the two groups were so different from one another, it was decided to try to form two parallel congregations, sharing the same facilities and some of the same events, but with separate organizations and separate worship services. The Khmers would be able to worship and carry out their business in their own language and according to their own customs. The original congregation would be able to retain some of its own style. Plans were made to hire a second staff person. The congregation asked both the district and the General Board for financial support. Merle Crouse was intrigued by the parallel congregation idea. It was a good way to combine Christian community with respect for cultural differences. It was a good direction for experimentation. Beyond that, the Antelope Park church was in great need. Both the district and the General Board committed money for the project.

The parallel congregation never developed. Late in 1982 and early in 1983 two large groups of refugees moved to California. The Khmers who were left, though still a sizable group, did not seem to want their own congregation. Antelope Park has stabilized at an attendance of 160 with many Khmers becoming permanent members of the congregation. The Antelope Park Brethren feel they can now handle all financial responsibilities, so in early 1984 the General Board and district new church development funds will end.

But the idea of two parallel congregations sharing the same building did not end there. It surfaced again in 1982 in the Pacific Southwest. There in Los Angeles, back in 1979, a Korean pastor named Dan Kim started a small independent congregation. This church met in homes until it grew too large. Pastor Kim approached Wayne Zunkel, pastor of the Panorama City Church of the Brethren and asked if his congregation could rent their church building for services. An agreement was reached, and as the two congregations shared space, the pastors worked together and began to find things in common. Wayne felt that the Korean fellowship might be at home in the Church of the Brethren. He invited the group to consider becoming a Brethren congregation. Pastor Kim did not give much thought to the invitation at first, but Wayne brought Howard Yu, a member of the McFarland congregation and a native of Korea, to talk to Dan Kim.

In Korea, Pastor Kim's church was the Korean Evangelical Church, which has no counterpart in the U.S. By joining the Brethren, he would break no formal denominational ties. Still the decision felt to him as though he were leaving that church. On the other hand, he had a sense that God wanted him to join the Church of the Brethren. He prayed about it, talked it over with his wife, and discussed it with his deacons. They entrusted the decision to him. In early 1982, he made his decision, and the congregation petitioned the Pacific Southwest Conference to be accepted as a Brethren congregation. At the October district conference, the petition was granted and the church became the Valley Korean Church of the Brethren, a full-fledged congregation. Pastor Kim's ordination was recognized. Both district and General Board funds were allocated to the new church. At present the membership stands at 50 and the weekly attendance at 40.

The worship services are in Korean. About half the members of the congregation speak English well. They are a closely-knit group. They have their own program and their own social events. But they also do things jointly with the Panorama City church. The members are seamstresses, gardeners, janitors; there is a postal worker, a chemical engineer. Many of the Koreans are well-educated but are forced into menial jobs because they do not speak English or have proper U.S. credentials. According to Pastor Kim, one of the members was vice-principal of a high school in Korea; now he is in real estate and the health food business. The members at Valley Korean tend to value work, order, industriousness, frugality, and a quiet, serious worship experience. Dan Kim is Bible-centered in his approach. "I emphasize Bible reading in the home and singing hymns," he says. "But also doing something. Don't just read it; follow it! If you want to start a church, push faith in the Bible. Without emphasizing biblical faith, it is impossible." Dan Kim talks about the importance of serving the Korean community, especially helping people to develop job skills. But he comes back to the Bible. "The Christian has to get power from the Bible. Then he can do the works."

The Koreans have a solid sense of morality and responsibility. This is one of the things they will share as they become part of the Church of the Brethren. Faith is a serious matter because it gives shape to life that must be lived in an alien culture.

The first church to begin in 1983 has a history that goes back to the 1976 feasibility study by Don Robinson in the Atlantic Northeast district. At that time the Mechanic Grove church considered the area around the town called Gap. There was a core of Mechanic Grove Brethren there who were anxious to have a church. The feasibility study, however, showed Lampeter to be a better site, and the people in Gap graciously gave way. Several years later, after Lampeter was well on its way, they began to talk again about a church. Another study was made by Don Robinson, and again it showed that Gap did not have significant growth potential. Don recommended an area in western Chester county to the east. But this time the Brethren in Gap would not be put off.

In 1982 and again in 1983, a Bible study series was conducted in the Gap area. Mechanic Grove took the initiative, as they did at Lampeter, with the district's support and counsel. When Mechanic Grove decided to begin meetings, the district provided a summer pastor. On June 5, 1983, the Gap fellowship held its first worship service in the Fairhaven School, which is an Amish school just east of Gap. Joel Nogle, the summer pastor, conducted the service and forty-two people attended.

The nucleus of this group comes from the Mechanic Grove and Conestoga congregations. There are a retired minister, a former associate pastor from Mechanic Grove, and several Sunday school teachers. Throughout its first seven months, the Gap fellowship averaged 33 people in attendance and more than $300 per week in giving. The district and the General Board have committed money for a full-time pastor, and the district is interviewing candidates as this is being written.

The Mechanic Grove Brethren have a talent for spawning new churches and giving them capable people from their own membership. When the Atlantic Northeast Brethren start a church, they seem to do it with strong lay leadership and part-time pastors. Having other large Brethren congregations nearby helps; they can provide pulpit supply, moral support, and even members. The district leaders are flexible enough to follow the initiative of a mother congregation or of a cluster of churches, as in the case of the Maine project. Working from these strengths, the Atlantic Northeast Brethren built a church at Lampeter and hope to build another at Gap.

In May of 1983, more than 60 people gathered in the conference facilities at New Windsor, Maryland, for a New Church Development Retreat—pastors, lay people from the new churches, district executives, and denominational leaders. It was a time to trade ideas, discuss problems, hear discussions of the steps in church development, see what other churches were doing, and be inspired. In the keynote address, Bob Neff, General Secretary, said, "I feel that what you represent and what the planting of new churches represents in the life of the Church of the Brethren is the new faith frontier for the church. My own experience has taught me that faithfulness is informed and forged by those new circumstances in which we find ourselves, which we can be only too little prepared for. In these new churches, we're wrestling with new situations where we're not so comfortable. There will be a new forging of faithfulness because of this unbelievable diversity."

Almost all the new church development in 1983 occurred in the two districts at the extreme ends of the Brotherhood, Pacific Southwest and Florida/Puerto Rico. At the same time that Pacific Southwest was accepting the Korean Church in 1982, it was beginning a project near San Diego. Several families in the San Diego church lived in the northern part of the county, a long distance from the church. Here new homes, shopping centers, fast food restaurants, and chain stores are spreading over the desert hills. It seemed to be an excellent place to start a church. Irven Stern, the pastor of the San Diego church, was enthusiastic about the idea. The district new church development committee was eager to move ahead. Glenn Stanford, an aggressive, capable pastor, who was serving the McFarland Congregation in the San Joachin Valley, was ready for a pastoral change and showed some interest in the project. The McFarland congregation, which has some strong supporters of new church work, offered to underwrite a large part of his salary. Everything seemed to fall into place. The district decided to give the go-ahead and to call Glenn Stanford to be the pastor. By September, 1982, Glenn and his family moved to Poway, the town selected as the base of operations.

At the same time Glenn was moving in, Wayne Fralin, at the district's request, conducted a feasibility study. Wayne's report was disturbing. Growth in that section of the county had slowed down, and the area was overchurched.

Nevertheless, Glenn began working with a list of Brethren in the area. As he contacted them, he acquainted himself with the community. Already in September he began to hold Bible studies in his home. On some nights there were as many as 10-12 people. But his explorations seemed to confirm Wayne Fralin's conclusions. Growth had slowed down. There were many small churches, some of them doing poorly. The ratio of churches to population was high. As the months passed he learned of six additional new fellowships launched just since his own arrival. Though this evidence was discouraging, Glenn kept working. He urged the new church development committee to let him begin regular worship. But the committee members were reluctant to take this next step.

In February of 1983 the committee asked Wayne Fralin to come back and do another study of other sections of the huge northern part of the county. This study showed that the Carlsbad area near the coast was a better location. At their meeting in May, the committee drove through Carlsbad and its environs, looking at the land developments and at possible church sites. Then in a session at a local restaurant they made a difficult decision—to close the Poway project and to begin again in Carlsbad.

Glenn Stanford supported this move, but it left him in an awkward position. The shift meant moving. Carlsbad was too far away to commute. The committee made it clear that Glenn was not obligated to move. If he was interested in staying with the north county project and starting over in the new location, they were open to that. If he did not want to do that, they would understand. The experience was painful for Glenn and his family. His decision finally was to leave the project and seek another pastorate. He resigned, and in September, 1983, he took a pastorate at the Garden City church in Kansas. The new church development committee called Glenn and Mary Frazier, who had been serving the Antelope Park church in Lincoln, Nebraska, and had been instrumental in the Khmer ministry. The Fraziers began their work in Carlsbad in November.

One of the most unusual new churches is an adopted congregation near Ponce, Puerto Rico. Ponce had been studied as a potential site before the Florida/Puerto Rico district shifted to Vega Baja. Not long after that decision, Jaime Rivera met a minister named Jorge Montes. Jorge was pastor of an independent church in Juana Diaz, a town just outside of Ponce in an area the district had originally surveyed. Jorge Montes liked what Jaime told him about the Brethren.

Jaime and his brother Jorge Rivera at Castañer liked what they saw and heard in Montes. His congregation seemed to fit into the hopes they have for the Church of the Brethren in Puerto Rico. They invited him to come to district conference in 1982. There he requested that the district sponsor his congregation. The district responded cautiously but with interest: Let's get acquainted with one another and study one another; then we'll talk further. A visit by a district delegation was planned for sometime in 1983.

There is a story connected with that visit. The group in Juana Diaz sets aside the month of January each year for prayer and renewal. They meet every night for the whole month. During January of 1983, their special prayer request was that the Brethren delegation would come that month. They were convinced that their prayer would be answered. As the month passed, Merle Crouse and Phyllis Carter, the district executive, became aware of the group's intense interest and a quick visit was scheduled for the end of the month. "I got there," Phyllis says, "and found out that they'd been in prayer since the first of January that we would act! And I had been reluctant to go! The plans were only confirmed on Thursday morning before we left on Friday. That's an awesome thing to know that God was having a people pray, and that happened!"

Jorge Montez, a short, stocky, restlessly energetic, athletic-looking man, tells his story. Before his dramatic conversion he was a successful engineer with plenty of money, an exciting lifestyle, and no interest in Christianity. The conversion separated him from his former life. He became active in the Catholic charismatic movement. Then he was drawn to the United Church (a Protestant denomination) because the people of this church stimulated him to study the Bible. Also he began to feel a call to the ministry, and he knew that because he was married he could not become a Catholic priest. After he joined the United Church, he was called to be pastor of the United Church congregation in Juana Diaz.

This congregation grew, and under his leadership it began to change its style. There has been a movement to "Latinize" worship in the former mission churches in Puerto Rico, to get away from the sedate hymns and restrained expression brought by North American missionaries, and to get back to the lively rhythms and language of the Latin culture. When this began to happen in Juana Diaz, the United Church split. Jorge Montes and many of the members were left without a building.

They continued to meet wherever they could find space. Eventually this became their pattern. Someone called them "Los Caminantes," which means "the walking ones," and the name stuck. They now use it as their church name. In 1983 when the Brethren from the district visited them, they were meeting in an open-air muffler shop.

Los Caminantes are a group of about 150 very active people, constantly on the move. They seem to do everything together. They meet often, they enjoy worship, they help one another. There is a constant hum of activity, but not dutiful activity. They seem to be having fun being Christians. There is a kind of delightful fertility about everything they do. But they are not disorganized. They have 10 commissions or departments to cover everything from Christian education to stewardship to drama and music. Their music is loud, lively, Latin, and very sophisticated. They have a singing group of seasoned entertainers and musicians, whose arrangements and renditions are almost professional in caliber. They use lead and backup singers, guitars, a bass, drums, guiros, maracas, and tambourines; and most of the songs they do are written by a member of the congregation.

When visitors come, they bring them up front and interview each one, using the microphone. Then the band and singers strike up a lively hymn; and while everyone sings, the members of the congregation come out of the pews and, one by one, go down the line hugging each visitor. After being hugged by dozens of people, the visitors are personally escorted back to their seats. If a visitor does not speak Spanish, the escort stays by to translate.

The worship is enthusiastic and loud, but in good order. Some members have charismatic gifts and some do not. The Bible is studied and referred to. The most obvious and overwhelming quality of the group is love. They come from all sorts of backgrounds and are like wanderers who have found a home with one another and are overjoyed. Yet they are not transient people in their personal lives. Many are well-educated and hold professional jobs. They support their pastor full-time.

The Brethren who visited them were charmed. Their worship and their warmth were contagious. But how would the more staid, reserved Brethren live with such an animated group? Indeed, that question may be asked of all Puerto Rico. Even the more sedate Castañer church has been using its organ less and guitars and güiros more. The Brethren on the Florida side of the district view the differences as an opportunity. They look for the vitality of the Puerto Rican churches to enliven the district. They do not seem to be afraid that by accepting their Puerto Rican Brethren they will lose their way. The district has encouraged the Puerto Rican churches to worship and operate in their own style, to be themselves.

The questions were not all on one side, however. Los Caminantes has a strong identity. They have been on their own for a long time. Would they feel comfortable with these reserved Brethren? Would the counsel and influence of the larger church be constricting? One of the things that impressed the folks from Los Caminantes was the way the Brethren conducted district meeting, strongly disagreeing and then coming together in fellowship. They were in accord with the Brethren emphasis on the New Testament and with the practice of the love feast. Not everyone could support the peace position, but many could. They sensed the Church of the Brethren would not try to coerce them in matters of faith.

The Brethren of the district felt this strong church would bring much needed leadership into the growing cluster of churches on the island. On October 15, 1983, Los Caminantes, with a membership of approximately 150, was accepted as a full congregation in the district of Florida/Puerto Rico.

People in the states tend to forget that Puerto Ricans are United States citizens, and Brethren tend to forget that Puerto Rico is not a foreign mission but part of the Brotherhood. Phyllis Carter says, "I expect the leadership we're developing in Puerto Rico to serve the whole Church of the Brethren. They are a parish. They are not a mission. I expect the Puerto Rico side of the district, because of their freshness, to call out and send out people. They are going to give us that first fresh experience of church, a Book of Acts experience of what church and church development is all about."

Just a day after Florida/Puerto Rico adopted Los Caminantes, the Pacific Southwest Conference adopted Bethel Temple Community church. In 1978 this black church, with a membership of approximately 100 and an attendance of 60-75, did not have a meeting place. The Pomona Church of the Brethren offered to rent them their facilities. For several years the two congregations shared the same space. James Washington, Bethel's pastor, a self-supporting minister who manages apartment building maintenance employees, became a close friend of Curtis Naylor, the Pomona pastor, and of Richard Landrum, who replaced Naylor in 1981. Gradually the two congregations became comfortable with one another and began to talk about getting together in some way.

In 1982 the Pomona congregation merged with the La Verne Fellowship church. When that process was completed and the La Verne Fellowship building was sold, serious talks began between Bethel Temple and Pomona, now called the Pomona Fellowship Church. Vernard Eller, professor of religion at the University of La Verne and a member of the church, taught a course on Brethren history for the Bethel members. The district executive, Truman Northup, was called into the discussion. Two models were considered: (1) Bethel Temple people would join the Pomona church; there would still be some separate events, but not two separate congregations. (2) There would be two Churches of the Brethren in the same building, which would interlock in selected ways; there would be separate organizations and worship services, but some shared events, such as Easter sunrise services, social gatherings, occasional worship services, and joint love feast celebrations. This second model was chosen. On October 15, 1983, the district unanimously voted to accept Bethel Temple Community Church of the Brethren as a full congregation.

According to Pastor Dick Landrum, the decision to live as two parallel congregations in the same facility establishes a delicate balance between separation, on the one hand, which could be labeled racist, and undifferentiated merger, on the other hand, which could ignore or obliterate worthwhile differences. The two groups seem to be satisfied with this balance. It allows them to enjoy the Christian fellowship they share yet continue to worship in the style that fits them.

In Florida/Puerto Rico at the same October meeting when Los Caminantes was adopted, the district accepted, as a fellowship, a Haitian group from Miami. This group was initiated by the First Church of the Brethren in Miami, a congregation that gives a home to people from many different cultures. Miami First, knowing this group of Haitians lived too far away to come regularly to the Church of the Brethren, encouraged them to begin meeting on their own. During Holy Week of 1983, they invited their Haitian friends to love feast. From that good experience together and others like it grew a request from the new group to become a Church of the Brethren.

The name of this new fellowship is Premiere Eglise Evangelique des Freres Haïtien Fellowship. Translated, that means First Haitian

Evangelical Church of the Brethren Fellowship. Ludovic St. Fleur was recognized as the pastor. His ministry is self-supported, but the district is assisting with funds for the congregation's meeting space and transportation. A district support committee was created. It is called in Creole, Comité Sipó Haïtien. The group meets in homes, and at the end of 1983 its average attendance was 35.

There is one last project which just got underway in 1983 and will have begun worship by the time this book is off the press. This church project has some new wrinkles. First, it will be financed in large part by mineral royalties accruing to a small congregation 180 miles away in another state. Second, it is in a place where there are no Churches of the Brethren, a distant sector of a district that is huge in area and small in number. Third, it is in a large planned community where church sites and church development are part of the overall plan. Fourth, it is pastored by a husband and wife team. And fifth, it is designed from the beginning to become a large multi-celled church, strong enough to start other churches throughout the large metropolitan area where it is situated. There are other new congregations hoping eventually to sponsor additional new churches, but The Woodlands is the only one with such a bold plan right from the start.

The congregation is Christ Our Peace Church of the Brethren in The Woodlands, a planned development north of Houston, Texas, in the far southern part of the Southern Plains district. The supporting congregation is a small but active church in Roanoke, Louisiana. The Roanoke church retained half of the mineral rights to a quarter section of land which it received in a will and then sold. Oil was discovered there, so the church now receives $5,000 per month for its share of the rights. This money would be more than enough to run their whole program, but instead of using it that way, the members have committed it to outreach. They are pledged to provide $1,000 per month to Christ Our Peace. When the time comes, they will give another $125,000 to the new church's building program. Roanoke has only 90 members and an average attendance of 39. The whole district has only 924 members and an average Sunday attendance of 373. Yet the district has pledged $28,000 per year, over a six-year period, to The Woodlands project. It's a bit like David's taking on Goliath—this tiny district and small church, planning not only a big church but a network of churches in huge, sprawling boomtown Houston.

The pastors are Timothy Jones and Jill Zook-Jones. Tim was the young United Church of Christ seminarian who gave that summer of leadership to help Lampeter get off the ground, who preached a sermon called "Grasshoppers in the Land of Giants," and who subsequently joined the Brethren. Jill served as summer intern under Earl Ziegler at Mechanic Grove. Tim completed a four-year stint at the Germantown Brick church in Virginia.

They began their work September 16, 1983. They have knocked on doors. They have started two Bible studies. They have invited people from the Bible study groups and from the community to help plan the first worship service which was held in February, 1984.

Tim and Jill attended a new church development workshop at Fuller Theological Seminary in California. They were encouraged to envision the size of the church they wanted right from the start. Because there are no Brethren churches near and because Houston is growing so rapidly, they believe a church of 350-400 people only makes sense, one strong enough to sustain itself and to reach out. They want their people to think of themselves not as a small intimate fellowship but as a growing congregation of small intimate fellowships. One Bible study is for people of all ages; one is a morning mothers group. These are not just gatherings to get people involved; they are the beginning of the church's subgroups.

The Woodlands project is a bold idea. Tim and Jill do not seem like "big growth" people. They don't have that slick, promoter's air about them. They seem properly modest and unassuming, as Brethren are expected to be; but they talk excitedly about their ambitious plans. It is a bit surprising, even refreshing, to hear someone who is properly "Brethren" talk without apology about large growth. By the standards of the rest of American Protestantism, 400 members is not a huge congregation, but it is a big dream for Brethren.

The story is not finished here, however. There are many new churches on the drawing boards, six months, a year, two years, maybe three years away. The Cranberry Township project, 30 miles north of Pittsburgh in the district of Western Pennsylvania, is interviewing for a pastor. This project is interesting because it is succeeding against strong opposition among the district leadership. The district of Northern Ohio is starting its second project, at Medina in the Cleveland area. The site is purchased. The pastor is being recruited. The plan is to have the pastor in place by September 1, 1984.

In Goshen, Indiana, in the Northern Indiana district, a group calling themselves the Communion Fellowship is seeking dual affiliation with Brethren and the Mennonite Church. Started as a student group on the Goshen College campus, it has grown to a membership of 55-60. It is interracial; many members are bilingual. It is an enthusiastic, evangelical group with lively worship and a strong, caring community. Merle Crouse says it is an Indiana version of Los Caminantes.

The district of Southern Ohio is planning a new church in Columbus. The Northview Church in Indianapolis is exploring the possibility of starting a church in the southern part of the city, with the support of the South/Central Indiana district. In Chesterfield County outside Richmond, Virginia, Virlina District will start its next church. They have purchased the lot and are now raising funds. They are also looking at lots and waiting for the right time to begin in Cary, North Carolina, in the Raleigh/Durham area. Florida/Puerto Rico is planning a church in the Greater Orlando area. Because their resources are stretched to the limit, they hope to do on the Florida side of the district what they have done on the Puerto Rico side and find another district to cosponsor the Orlando project.

A church development committee in Western Plains district is looking at the Colorado Front Range area, where they plan to start two projects; they are in the fund-raising stage. The Mid-Atlantic district is giving consideration to a new church in Washington, D.C. There is a possibility of adopting a Hispanic church in Los Angeles, California. The Pacific Southwest Conference is taling about a new church in Mesa, Arizona, where a group of Brethren meet in the winter months. In Idaho a group of 12 people from the Nampa church have made a covenant to start a new church in the South Meridian area and have the blessing of the district of Idaho. And in California, the Modesto congregation is working to start a Hispanic fellowship.

And so, here at the beginning of 1984, the new church development movement is gaining momentum at a bewildering rate. Phyllis Carter says, "The Spirit is moving and we have nothing to do. We are doing our feasibility studies, doing our homework, but the truth is it's all being done by the grace of God. I think that's true clear across the church. I don't know what's going to happen next, and that's what makes it exciting. I know something's going to happen next!"

CHAPTER FOUR
THE NEW BRETHREN

Why Is This Happening?

There is a feeling among Brethren that the church must grow. Like the urges lying behind any group effort, the feeling is complex. But it has at least two components. One is the anxiety caused by our diminishing membership. The other is the sense that the Brethren have something to offer.

On the purely human level, these are good motives. In our society, growth is a sign of life, whether we are talking about the auto industry, the Lions Club, or the church. A warning bell does ring in Brethren heads, reminding us that following Christ sometimes means being unpopular and losing members, but we tend to believe this is true only of the short run. Over the long haul, we expect growth. Besides, there is nothing about our diminishing membership that indicates it has been caused by unpopular stands we have taken. We sense that it is happening because we have done something wrong or not done something right or simply done nothing. It is time for a new start.

Our society also encourages us to believe that it is of value to have something to offer. It is good to know who you are and what you have to give. We sense that we have been apologetic for ourselves as Brethren. We must be positive about ourselves. More than that, if we look closely, we see much to feel good about. Why haven't we been offering our convictions, our traditions, and our special values more aggressively?

Both of these impulses are natural. They are to be expected.

Organizations go through cycles, and the Brethren are on the up side of the cycle. To minimize this or rationalize it with "spiritual" explanations would be hypocritical.

But to say natural causes are the whole explanation would be wrong too. There is also something else at work here. Brethren believe that as Christians we are called to make a witness. Oddly, we do not agree on what the witness is. The Brethren in Maine would not say and do what the Brethren in Blacksburg would say and do. But they would agree that a Christian is called to say and do something, and further they would agree that the Brethren have a unique witness. This is different from having something to offer that makes us feel good. This is the call to go and preach and baptize and serve, even if it does not always feel good. In this sense, though, we are not being called to anything new. We have always had the great commission before us.

There are other Brethren who sense still another cause for this burst of activity. They believe that God is moving to renew the Church of the Brethren and that the new church development movement might be to the years ahead what some of the great movements of our history were to years past. They believe God has a purpose for Brethren. There is not much talk of this because Brethren are not quick to justify themselves with appeals to a special providence, but there is a sense of the auspiciousness of this moment.

From the Grass Roots

Whatever Brethren may say or feel or believe about this movement, one thing is certainly remarkable about it. It did not get started by denominational decision. It has not been directed by a denominational board. It did not grow, at least initially, by cross-fertilization. Gordon Bucher in Northern Ohio was surprised when he found his district in the midst of a flurry of activity. Almost every project grew out of someone's need or someone's vision. The roots of almost all the projects go back to the mid-seventies, when there was no movement at all and no talk of new church development.

I cannot see any obvious connection between these events. The only person who has been in touch with every project is Merle Crouse. As important as his role has been, he did not plant the seeds. The idea for Trinity came from a district committee. The idea for Lampeter came from Sadie Kreider, a lay person. The idea for Lewiston came from Jim Myer, a minister. The idea for Good

Shepherd in Blacksburg came from district executive Owen Stultz and others in the district. The idea for Genesis came from the dreams of three seminarians. If you press these people, they will say yes they felt it was time to do something, and if you press them a little harder, they will say they felt the spirit of God moving in their idea.

It is a measure of the vitality of this movement that it sprang up so spontaneously. It was not organized from the top. In our history the things that have changed our denomination did not come down from above. They started in the convictions and actions of individuals and sometimes small groups. They were debated in Annual Conferences. The boards and offices that have become our General Board and General Offices grew up to implement them. But they came from somewhere in the grass roots. This is consistent with the way the Gospel was given. Jesus was one man preaching to a few hundred people in small villages. Paul and the apostles were a handful of people starting tiny churches in widely scattered cities. This new church development movement is a handful of little fellowships, some of them scattered in, what are for Brethren, out-of-the-way places. What will they grow into?

Leadership's Role

Denominational leadership, however, has been involved, and how it has been involved is one of the notable features of the movement. The General Board hired a staff person and provided money. The General Secretary and the Parish Ministries Commission have supported new church development. Annual Conference regularly receives reports on its progress. *Messenger*, the denominational monthly, features it. But there has been no attempt to control it. It is as though our central leadership is a bit surprised it is happening but is glad for it, and until something goes wrong is not going to tamper with it.

Merle Crouse is the only person at the national level completely identified with the movement. Yet he has not tried to control it or even organize it highly. He really has no authority to do so. He has worked quietly, often behind the scenes, as a consultant. His power is in persuasion, in his useful knowledge, in his savvy, and in the money his office can allocate. There is power, of course, in this money, but none of the projects is so dependent on it that it could not proceed without it. Even the location of Merle's office has helped decentralize the movement. When he left the Florida/Puerto Rico district position and gave up his Latin America responsibilities to be full-time church development consultant, he did not move back to Elgin, Illinois, where the headquarters are. He kept his office in Florida.

Maybe the key to Merle's style lies in his foreign mission work earlier in his career. He began his work in Ecuador in 1959 at a time when Brethren were beginning to "indigenize" overseas programs. Then when he was based back in Elgin, he was in charge of all church development throughout the foreign mission field at a time when indigenization was proceeding rapidly. You might say he practices indigenization here at home in new church work. This means respecting local initiative, keeping power and responsibility in local hands, seeing local peculiarities as strengths, and believing that the gospel takes root in different ways among different people. Keep a low profile; use power sparingly; let others take the credit. Encourage people's ambitions and dreams. Step back and stay away when no longer needed. This is Merle's style.

Diversity

A marked feature of this movement is its diversity. The Lewiston Brethren would not feel comfortable with the Cape Coral Brethren. The Lampeter Brethren and the Juana Diaz Brethren would be frustrated if they had to worship together regularly. The church in Vermont would not succeed in Houston. The Haitian Brethren from Miami would be strange to the Bethel Temple Brethren from Pomona. The loudspeakers and Latin music at Vega Baja would never fit at Blacksburg.

This diversity is all the more confusing because the differences are in matters of theology, culture, race, polity, and practice. If there were one or two factors constant and the rest varied, it would be easier to fathom. If, for instance, all members of the new churches were white middle-class Americans, but with theological differences, it would be easier to see why they might be together. Or if the new churches had people of different racial, ethnic, and cultural backgrounds who were all evangelicals, or if everyone were equally committed to peace and social justice despite all other differences —then this conglomeration of churches would make sense. But there does not seem to be any common thread—except perhaps that the Brethren are nice people and will accept almost anyone.

Putting it that way is putting it negatively: the Brethren have no tough convictions; they are pleasant, bland people who will go along with anything. Certainly someone could look at this assortment of churches and make that accusation.

But made as an observation, not as an accusation, the statement has some truth. The Brethren are nice people. The Brethren are willing to accept people. Perhaps that's the beginning of something new and good. Merle Crouse says that the story of Peter and Cornelius in Acts is where we have to look to understand the new churches. The sheet that was let down in Peter's dream was filled with a great variety of strange creatures. Peter took this to mean that the gentiles were no longer unclean. The Jewish Christians began to accept gentiles into the church, and the church began to change—and it began to grow. Are the Brethren finally letting the "gentiles" in?

The question seems strange. The acculturation process for the Brethren began 130 years ago. The history of that period is the story of how we became part of the world from which we once separated ourselves. We took ideas from the world. We sought education in the world. We went out to convert the world. We went out to serve the world. We began to enjoy worldly things. We began to feel at home in the world. We came to love and respect the people of the the world. But we never invited them in.

If you look at us, despite all the changes we have undergone, we are still mostly a group of middle-class whites with Germanic last names. We seem to do better with the people of the world when we are on their turf than when they are on ours. (This, some say, is where the new church development movement in the fifties and sixties foundered. The Brethren were not really ready to let in people who were different.) Perhaps this new church movement will change that. Perhaps this is the next step in our development. Now that we have let in the ideas and needs and problems of the world, maybe we will let in its people.

At the moment the movement seems colorful and exciting. But suppose more Korean Americans want to join us in Los Angeles? Suppose Puerto Rico blossoms with Churches of the Brethren? Suppose Germantown succeeds and Bethel Temple grows and the Haitian church flourishes? Suppose we begin to have churches in Hispanic neighborhoods. Suppose more and more people in our churches come from other denominational backgrounds? Suppose we begin to see black faces in the delegate body or on standing committee at Annual Conference? Suppose someone named Rivera or Hong becomes Moderator of Annual Conference? These are not simply rhetorical questions. If this new church movement continues, there will be real changes. Some of them are occurring already in Pacific Southwest and Florida/Puerto Rico.

What Can We Learn?

It is easy and interesting to speculate about the impact these new churches will have on the denomination. But congregations, whether they are new and unusual or old and typical, have a life of their own, apart from questions of denominational identity. The new congregations are alive and vital. What can we learn from them?

First, the experience of Christian community is fresh, exciting, intimate, and full of purpose. People are in a new church because they want to be there. They are enthusiastic and committed. They are not burdened by old ways of doing things. They can experiment. They cannot assume that they know what's on each other's mind just because they have gone to church together for many years. They have to get to know one another. They have a purpose—to help the church grow. They have to be willing to give time and money. They can't slip into the background. There is no "deadwood." The group is small; it's easy to know everyone. There is an environment where people can grow and where the Spirit can move. We are reminded that the New Testament churches were small and new.

Second, there seems to be a more immediate sense of God's active personal presence in the congregation. God is leading individuals and God is directing the church. In a congregation where everything runs smoothly, God can be forgotten. In a new church everything is uncertain. There is more need for faith.

Third, we learn that Christians do not need a church building, a large membership, a fully developed program, or a full-time pastor to find spiritual satisfaction. While the new churches move toward these goals, some of the greatest and best moments are in the early days of struggle. The Lampeter Brethren still talk fondly of the fire hall. They were crowded together on metal chairs. When someone was absent, they noticed the empty space. There was one door, and people could not get in and out without greeting one another. The pastor always stood behind a table with a lectern; he was on the same level as the congregation and almost on top of them. Now they are in a beautiful, spacious building and are doing very well, but some of the old closeness has been lost—that feeling that they were in it together, bucking tough odds.

The goals of new church developers are usually to see the new congregations on a solid footing like the old, established ones. But maybe our established congregations should be prodded into situations where they have to struggle like the new ones. Maybe they ought to be challenged to start daughter congregations like Mechanic Grove did. Maybe a new church ought to think not so much about getting over the hump to self-support as about becoming strong enough to start another church. I suggest this not because I think numerical growth is important but because Christians seem to be more alive when they struggle, when they have to act on their faith, when they worship in small groups, and when their bills aren't fully paid. Perhaps the importance of this new church development movement does not lie in the numbers of new churches and new people we are adding but in what they can teach us about being alive in Christ.

Different From the Past

One of the oft-repeated observations about new church work today in the Church of the Brethren is that it is different from church extension work of the 1950s and 1960s. This observation often comes from people who were involved both then and now. They generally cite four things: (1) the leadership is more experienced; (2) the planning is better; (3) the funding is more adequate; (4) the community church model is working this time. There have been no comparative studies done to confirm these observations, but let's look at them because they give us further insight into this present work.

First, on the matter of leadership, it has been said often that the pastor/developers of the earlier period were frequently inexperienced. The new churches were "plum" projects for those just out of seminary. At least three of the present pastor/developers and one steering committee chairperson were pastors in that earlier work at the beginning of their careers. Today, experienced pastors are placed in the new churches, people like Don Shank or Norman Harsh, each with more than 20 years experience in a variety of churches.

Second, the planning is carefully done. A feasibility study establishes the community and often the site. The district creates a new church development committee and then usually a steering committee for the new fellowship. The district plans a fund-raising campaign. Merle Crouse gives consultation. At the right time the General Board pledges funds. District people are kept informed. The district executive coordinates the work. The pastor is recruited and sent to a church development workshop. He does not rush into the first worship service. He gets well-acquainted with the community. He gathers a core group. Only then does the church begin.

Wherever this process has been followed carefully, the church has gotten off to a good start. The key person in the planning and execution is the district executive. He makes sure that the process works, that the right committees are set up, that the idea is handled properly by district board and district conference, that the denominational consultant is called in when needed. He oversees the pastoral search. In districts where the district executive is not well-organized and is struggling to keep up with events rather than shaping them, new church development has suffered. It is possible for a district to start one church successfully without strong leadership from the district executive, but it is extremely difficult to have several projects and an overall strategy. The district executive has to be in the middle of it.

The third thing being done right is the financial planning. I have heard it said that in the 1950s the goal was to get a building up as soon as possible and then expect people to come and fill it up. This time the building comes late and only when the new group can handle it. But planning for the building starts early. Ideally, the site is bought and paid for by the district, and the major funds are raised before the pastor arrives. This signals to the community and to the new members that the district is serious about the project. A financial plan is worked out that includes contributions from the district (the largest share), from the General Board, and from the new fellowship itself. The first two diminish year by year as the third increases. The district commits itself to a large outlay when the building is constructed, and the General Board promises a grant and a loan. These amounts are adjusted so that the new church is not burdened by its finances but still has a challenge. In the four cases where a building has been built, these projections have been fairly accurate. Lampeter was perhaps given too much money, and Trinity was not given quite enough, but these errors did not result in serious problems.

The fourth difference is the most fundamental. I have often heard it said that in the earlier church extension work the new churches were caught between being community-oriented churches, thus down-playing or even apologizing for Brethren peculiarities, and being traditional Churches of the Brethren, thus tending to give "non-Brethren" people the feeling they were outsiders. There is no evidence of that in this movement. The new churches seem to be equally comfortable welcoming strangers and lifting up Brethren values.

Quite often in the earlier days a Brethren core was considered desirable. Now, it is generally avoided. Norman Harsh made a point of not going after the Brethren in Blacksburg. He wanted a church of people who were there because of desire or need or calling, not background. Where attempts have been made to gather scattered Brethren, the results have been disappointing. The Boston fellowship and the GBAF are cases in point.

There is only one church that began with a sizable Brethren core; that was Lampeter. But these Brethren were active, outgoing members of a vital church. They were not Brethren who had long been inactive. They lived in the area and wanted a church. They quickly welcomed and involved people from other backgrounds, even electing one to head the church board. So it is possible to start with a Brethren core. The question is what kind of core is it? Do these Brethren really want a church and why?

Models

The community church is the model Brethren are using most frequently and most successfully. In 1983, a Manual for Church Planters, called *Developing New Congregations in the Church of the Brethren*, was published by the General Board. In this manual, this model is described as a "community-oriented church in a new town." Christ the Servant, Good Shepherd in Bradenton, Trinity, Lampeter, Good Shepherd in Blacksburg, Fellowship in Christ, Christ Church in Carol Stream, Gap, Christ Our Peace in Houston, and Cristo el Senor fit this model or are variations on it. They are placed in growing areas. They try to reach new members as they move in. The church site is in a high traffic area. They employ or plan to employ a full-time pastor. They need to reach a membership of at least 200 to support their program. They are sponsored by a district.

The second model identified in the Manual for Church Planters is called the "discipleship/Brethren identity church." This kind of congregation tends to have a more rigorous understanding of what it means to be Brethren. The Lewiston and Genesis churches are examples. This church may locate in a neighborhood or city that does not have a promising growth pattern. It may choose a place where Brethren are unknown and may not easily fit in. It will begin with bivocational leadership or the free ministry. It will not start with a site. It will not have immediate plans for a building. As a result, costs for leadership and facilities will be kept low. Several families may relocate to form a nucleus for the church. The growth will be more modest than in the community church model and will not be as necessary, since financial obligations will be fewer. The group may eventually purchase and renovate an older building. The sponsor may be a district, a congregation, or a cluster of congregations.

All new churches wish to establish both a visible institution and a witness, but the difference between the community church model and the discipleship model is that the one tries to establish the institution so that the witness can be made and the other aims to establish the witness so the institution might grow. It is a difference in emphasis. In the latter case, a place can be chosen where the witness is needed even if the demographics are unpromising. The project has to be leaner. The money is spent as a witness, not as an investment. The sponsor is prepared for the risk. For the community church, the location must have feasibility. A great deal of money is spent with the expectation of a return—a substantial church with a good facility and with a large enough membership that, in time, will support the programs of the district and the Brotherhood as well as make a mark in the community.

By this analysis, Lewiston and Genesis easily fit the discipleship/Brethren identity model, but they differ from each other in their attitude toward membership. The Genesis project is like the community church in that it will accept members where they are. They do not ask people to conform to their ways. On the other hand, the Lewiston Brethren make well-defined demands on new members.

These churches also differ in the way they make their witness. The Lewiston Brethren have explained who they are and have staunchly held to their ways, but they have not regularly called attention to their witness. The Genesis Brethren have sought publicity. Dick Shreckhise has commented that they have become one of the best-known churches in the area. When they are interviewed for the newspaper, they welcome the opportunity to talk about peace, to explain the love feast, to discuss Brethren heritage. They want people to know who the Brethren are and what they stand for. In letting people know their identity as a church, they have been the most aggressive of all the new churches. Others have thoroughly advertised their presence, especially the community churches that need to grow, but the Genesis Brethren have advertised their witness.

A comparison of Lewiston and Genesis is so interesting because of what it teaches us about the Brethren. The Brethren Revival Fellowship is correct when it says the Brethren have departed from our old ways, though what they call our "old ways" are really the way we were near the beginning of this century and not at the beginning of our history. But they are right. The Church of the Brethren has changed dramatically in this century. In New England, the Lewiston Brethren are trying to create a Church of the Brethren as it was before the changes, and the Genesis Brethren are trying to create a Church of the Brethren as it can be now that it has survived all those changes. In between these two visions of the church, Brethren took off their plain clothing, sought education, acquired a trained professional ministry, abandoned church discipline, moved to the suburbs, joined the civil rights movement and the anti-war movement, became politicized, indigenized their missions, stopped being evangelistic, developed a worldwide service program, and began to feel at home in the world.

The remarkable thing is that at first glance these two fellowships look so much alike. They both went to New England where the Brethren have never been, and they did this against the prevailing wisdom that churches should go where the growth is.

The third model for new church development is the "church that becomes Brethren by adoption." This is an independent group looking for a denominational home. It has members, has its own pastor, and has doctrines, practices, and an outlook congenial to the Brethren. The pastor may be bi-vocational or full-time. It may or may not have a building. There is a careful process of mutual investigation and negotiation. The new group agrees to be oriented to the history, beliefs, and practices of the Brethren, to accept our polity, and to support our program. Good Shepherd in Bradenton, Valley Korean, Bethel Temple, Los Caminantes, and, to a lesser extent, Premiere Eglise Evangelique des Freres Haïtien Fellowship are examples.

That these churches are coming to the Church of the Brethren is the most unusual feature of this new church development movement. Nothing like this has ever happened to the Brethren. Why are they coming? There are the obvious reasons. We are flexible and hospitable. We are willing to learn as well as teach. We welcome dialogue. We ask a new church to take our ways seriously, but we don't push them. In our polity, neither Annual Conference nor the district can dictate to a local church. We tolerate great variety in our body. Viewed from the vantage point of a congregation looking for a home and uneasy about what it might have to give up or undergo, those qualities must look pretty good. Dan Kim, the pastor of Valley Korean, says, "The Church of the Brethren is like its word—Brethren. Kindness. Also humility. For example, I went to district conference. They accepted me. They stood up and clapped. Each person shook my hand or embraced me. My heart was warmed. This is a great strength."

Adoption also has a benefit for the Brethren. The advantage does not lie in gaining people or congregations; it lies in the enlarged community we become. Blacks, Hispanics, and Asians do not readily join our congregations. We do not do well starting churches in their neighborhoods. Of the five churches we have adopted, four fall into one of those categories. Adoption is a shortcut to cultural diversity. By learning to live with groups of people who are different from us, we may begin to feel more comfortable with them when they come to our congregations one by one.

Cristo el Señor in Vega Baja could be added to the adoption list, though the Brethren helped start it. Jaime Rivera, the pastor, explains why people in Puerto Rico come to the Brethren. "The way that the Brethren work is much different from the way other denominations work. For example, the Brethren wanted to receive this project and help. Then we can help the Brethren later. The people say, 'I don't see other denominations working that way.' People are going to support that kind of church. They see there is not so much interest just to make membership. Other denominations put pressure on: 'Have numbers, then we give you money.'"

Jaime goes on, "This church is going to be a community church. We are interested in social work. It is a balance—the social work and the spiritual work. You cannot separate them. The Church of the Brethren works that way. People here see that." Luigi Perez also regards this as a chief difference of the Brethren. Other churches in Puerto Rico do not do service work. Merle Crouse thinks that this will make the Church of the Brethren an attractive church on the island. In addition to churches we start, Merle expects more congregations like Los Caminantes to come to us. The Brethren need to be prepared. As this is being written, a field director is being recruited for Puerto Rico. "The right person there for the next five or ten years could proliferate the churches," Merle says. "We'd have fifteen churches! And the leaders would pop out of the communities. But we need to keep training them and bringing them together, shaping the church. There's a fullness of time in Puerto Rico! There's no doubt about it!"

Is there a "fullness of time" for the Brethren not only in Puerto Rico but in the Pacific Southwest as well? Wayne Zunkel, pastor of the Panorama City church where Valley Korean shares the building, claims there are as many as 50 more independent Korean congregations in the Los Angeles area who need a denominational home. Is the Church of the Brethren called to be a global church, not overseas but here at home? This adoption process bears watching.

The fourth model presented in The Manual is called the "racial/ethnic minority church." This is the most problematic of the four models, the one at which Brethren are least successful. We do well when we adopt a church in this category. Valley Korean and Bethel Temple are examples. But we have difficulty *starting* a new church in an "ethnic" neighborhood. The Germantown church would be an example.

This difficulty may account for the fact that the model is not well-defined in the Manual for Church Planters. The other three models refer to a style or approach; this refers to the kind of people who make up the church. Theoretically, any one of the other three models could be used to create a "racial/ethnic minority church." And as indicated above, several of the churches that fit the "adoption" model fit this model too. What we really need is a fourth approach designed for the inner city or for a changing neighborhood or for a place where people are economically deprived or socially isolated, a model for *starting* a church in such a place, which is a much different matter from adopting one.

What Is Feasible?

The model that works best for the Brethren is the community church. It is not hard to see why. We are typically middle-class folk, upwardly mobile, well educated, and increasingly more urban. Even in the churches that are still in rural areas, there are fewer farmers and more people working in business, industry, education, and community services. We are the kind of people who live in nice subdivisions. Brethren, for the most part, plan their lives well, become solid, productive members of the community, eventually buy a house, and acquire a mortgage. The new churches we are starting tend to be well-planned; they establish themselves solidly in the community; they eventually build a church facility; and they acquire a mortgage.

This observation can be taken as a criticism. It can also be taken as evidence that Brethren are doing what we do best. And in so doing, we are countering the materialism, nationalism, and alienation in middle-class life with our convictions on the simple life, peace, and community. So when we start a church in Blacksburg, Massillon, or Carol Stream, we are going where we fit in and where we can have an impact.

To find these places, we do feasibility studies. But feasibility is based on sociological criteria. We know that we are called to be something more than sociologically astute. We know we are called to be more than just feasible. This is why the fact that the churches we start are "community churches" is so important. Through them people from all backgrounds come to us. This also is why the churches we adopt are so important. With them we are carried beyond what we do well or where we are comfortable. We are thrust into brotherhood that is broader and potentially deeper than our own familiar Brotherhood. With new Brethren we become Brethren in a new way.

Do We Want to Grow?

I observed at the beginning of this chapter that some Brethren have the feeling that the church needs to grow. But many Brethren have mixed feelings about growth. We want it but not too much of it. That makes me ask the question: Do we really want to grow? The Church of the Brethren has 169,000 members. Would we want the church to double its size? Would we want it to have a half-million members, a million members? I'm not suggesting that we should want that. I'm trying to get at our psychology. I. Harvey Brumbaugh, president of Juniata College for many years at the beginning of this century, used to call Juniata a "right little, tight little college." Are we a "right little, tight little denomination"? If we are, then we have here a movement that will peter out after 40 or 50 churches. We will begin to feel uneasy, slow down, and stop. We won't say that's what we are doing, but we'll do it.

And maybe that's what we should do. Perhaps we should start 40 or 50 churches every 20 years to stir us up a bit, bring in some new ideas, keep up our numbers, and go on making our witness as best we can, concentrating on service and peace with a burst of renewal from the charismatic side every so often and a tug or two back to our roots from the Anabaptist side. Nothing excessive, mind you, just good, solid, friendly Brethren Christianity. The question is not whether the Church of the Brethren as we know it is good or bad. The question is,

Will we insist upon it? Will we cling to it? How open are we? If we are called to grow, will we?

One thing observation can show us is that we are not organized for growth. Our congregations are organized to run smoothly and to serve the members and often the community but not to bring people in or to start daughter fellowships. We do not have our own training program for pastor/developers. We do not have books and pamphlets designed for new people nor for adopted congregations. We do not have materials in Spanish or Korean. We do not train seminarians in church development. Even among the new churches, only Christ Our Peace in Houston and the churches in Puerto Rico and New England have as a part of the initial plan to start more churches as soon as they are on their feet. In the other new churches there is the unspoken feeling that once the new congregation is a solid, self-sufficient Church of the Brethren the job is done.

I am not advocating these measures. As a matter of fact, they make me a bit uncomfortable. I mention them because without them this movement will not last. The people who are really excited about new church development will have soon taken us about as far as we can go. To go further, we will have to change both our attitudes and our institutions. So the question remains: Are we willing to grow, how much, and in what ways?

It is interesting that what we have here is new church development and not evangelism. Presumably, if we wanted to grow for growth's sake, personal evangelism would be the quickest way. For instance, if every congregation added 20 members next year, we would increase by 20,000 people. We have never had an increment of increase like that. Yet 20 new members for each congregation does not seem impossible. On the other hand, if we take the churches we have already started and if we continue to start five churches every year through 1990, we will have something over 50 new churches. If we assume that each one will reach 200 members eventually, we will have added approximately 11,000 members by sometime in the 1990s. This figure does not allow for the fact that not all of the churches will reach 200 members (nearly half of our old, established congregations now have fewer than 100 members), nor does it allow for the fact that some of those members will come from other Churches of the Brethren. So if we are thinking of growth in numbers, an evangelism strategy would be more effective and cost less. But starting new churches seems to fit us better than expanding our old ones.

Actually, congregational growth and new church development do not exist apart from one another. For Mechanic Grove, starting two new churches has stimulated its own growth. If the new church development movement continues, one of its effects may be to stimulate growth in the congregations supporting it.

What Do We Have to Offer?

I also observed at the beginning of this chapter that Brethren feel they have something to offer. What is that? What are our strengths? We have a strong sense of community. We approach the Bible seriously, but we do not follow it slavishly, nor do we interpret it literally. (Though we probably no longer read it as much as we used to or ought to.) We tend to be quiet about our personal relationship with God and talk more readily about peace and service and social justice. We have trouble putting personal faith and social action together, but we are doing better. If anything, we are shifting our emphasis a bit from the latter to the former, to personal spiritual renewal. But nonetheless, our peace witness is strong; our service work is constant. We believe that you have to live your faith, not just talk about it. We are a warm church. We care. Some have said we have humility. We are active in the community.

We don't need to claim we have all of the truth in order to say that the truth we have has claims on people. We can preach the gospel without being exclusive. We do not judge the person who has no interest in the church or in Christianity, leaving that judgment to God. We are thus able to enjoy relationships with non-Christians without feeling that our first responsibility is to convert them. We respect people and cultures that are different from ours.

We have a polity that encourages involvement at all levels. Our love feast is a strong and vital symbol of our faith and our life together. In this day of televised Christianity we have something that is refreshing. Our experience of Christ is quiet and undramatic. We are more likely to hear a still, small voice than have a vision. When you press most Brethren, you will find they have a simple, everyday faith that God is near and cares. This is especially true for the "ordinary" people in our churches. And though our leaders are good, our real strength lies in these people—solid, honest, somewhat unimaginative, open-minded, faithful, unpretentious, and ready to serve. Certainly if the spirit of God chose to move among a group of people with these qualities, something good could be done.

An End and a Beginning

One hundred and thirty-three years ago, Henry Kurtz began to print "The Gospel Visitor," the first Brethren periodical. From that monthly and the ideas that were discussed in it came dozens more periodicals and a large publishing program. Then came higher education, the Sunday school movement, evangelistic meetings, foreign missions, and, in this century, the theological seminary, the trained ministry, the social gospel, the national offices, worldwide service projects, and the social activism of the 60s and 70s. There has been an unbroken chain of change. Throughout this whole time we have looked outside ourselves for our cues. And through the whole period our denominational leaders have always been leading the way.

I think it could be argued that this period has come to an end. Publishing is no longer central to our denominational life. Our six colleges are virtually independent of the church, and the majority of our youth go elsewhere to college. Our Sunday schools are rather moribund, and Sunday school work does not command the attention it once did. Our foreign missions have been indigenized. Our service work is strong, but we do it quietly. Our seminary is fully developed and has a high standing. Our ministry is trained. Our national offices are in time of change and uncertainty. We continue to be concerned about peace and social issues but they are not the rallying points they once were.

And that's really the issue. In the past we have always had a rallying point, something to work on. We knew where we were going. But for some years now we have not had that. We can no longer look outside of ourselves as we used to do. Our acculturation process is complete. We can't look to our denominational leaders because we've caught up with them. The people in our congregations are no longer less sophisticated or less well educated than our leaders. Where do we go next?

Maybe this new church development movement is the next thing. It forces us to look inward to the strengths God has given us, not outward to the next item on the world's agenda. Maybe now that we're finally and fully in the mainstream of American life, it's time we had something to say to it, something of a decidedly spiritual nature that goes beyond peace and social justice to the heart of the gospel of love that makes peace possible and justice real. Maybe we are called to start churches all over this land. Maybe we are called to accept all kinds of people even if it means giving up some of the coziness of our family. Maybe the church is at a turning point that will affect us as deeply and change us as completely as the events that issued from Henry Kurtz's printing press. Perhaps like the gospel that was hidden in obscure villages when Jesus started his ministry, the gospel that is hidden in these new churches is going to spread among us and beyond us.